TRANSFORMING

CONFLICT AND ANGER

INTO PEACE

AND NONVIOLENCE

TRANSFORMING

CONFLICT AND ANGER

INTO PEACE

AND NONVIOLENCE

A Spiritual Direction

Janet Malone

NOVALIS

© 2007 Novalis, Saint Paul University, Ottawa, Canada

Cover design and layout: Pascale Turmel
Cover image: © PhotoDisc

Business Offices:

Novalis Publishing Inc.
10 Lower Spadina Avenue, Suite 400
Toronto, Ontario, Canada
M5V 2Z2

Novalis Publishing Inc.
4475 Frontenac Street
Montréal, Québec, Canada
H2H 2S2

Phone: 1-800-387-7164
Fax: 1-800-204-4140
E-mail: books@novalis.ca
www.novalis.ca

Library and Archives Canada Cataloguing in Publication

Malone, Janet
    Transforming conflict and anger into peace and nonviolence : a spiritual direction /
Janet Malone.

Includes bibliographical references.
ISBN 978-2-89507-692-6

    1. Anger–Religious aspects–Christianity. 2. Interpersonal
conflict--Religious aspects–Christianity. I. Title.

BV4627.A5M34 2007   241'.3   C2007-900363-X

Printed in Canada.

We acknowledge the financial support of the Government of Canada through the Book
Publishing Industry Development Program (BPIDP) for our publishing activities.

5   4   3   2   1   10   09   08   07

With love and gratitude:

To the memory of my parents, Nellie and Leo, and my dear sister Rosemary,

and

to my siblings Dan, Eileen, Jerry, Linda and Ray

ACKNOWLEDGMENTS

Deep gratitude to Clemmie McCarron, CND, and the other members of the Provincial Team of the then St. Joseph Province who, in the 1980s, asked me to go back to school to do doctoral studies. My "yes" to your request of leaving the known and successful to move into the unknown continues to be such a gift. The rest, as they usually don't say, is "herstory."

Indebted to each of my Salesian friends at Elmthorpe. You welcomed me so graciously into your midst while I was at Oxford University doing research on this project. A special thank you to you, Sr. Bridget, for the use of your printer when mine refused to work post shipping to the UK, and none could be found that was compatible with my computer.

Recognition of my colleague Canon Vincent Strudwick, at Oxford. I so respected your thoughtful reading of the initial manuscript of this book. Your comments helped with its maturation.

Finally, acknowledgment of all the people in the different groups, institutions and organizations (academic, business, civic, religious), courageous enough to take a course, a workshop, a training session to (re)learn how to transform your conflict and anger energies in nonviolent ways. It has been a privilege working with and learning from you. Your practical wisdom suffuses these pages.

CONTENTS

FOREWORD

Anger and conflict come from wounds. None of us deserves our wounds – neither the wounds inflicted by a suicide bomber or jet fighter nor the invisible, decades-old wounds of a heart denied emotional nourishment as a baby.

My own mother's wounds were expressed in periods of anger and depression. Her chronic state of fear forced me to face myself and to come to a place of deeper healing, peace and even joy. But my primal experience of my mother's fear and anger and depression created in me a heart with "unfinished business," a heart yearning to heal the wounds behind whatever anger and conflict I encountered. So I recognize the risk-taking work done around anger and conflict as being central to the work of nonviolence.

Anger is energy that is both dangerous and sacred. We can waste this God-given energy or learn to transform it for healing and for the growth of the life force of nonviolence. Conflict is natural and inevitable. Avoidance or denial of conflict has nothing to do with nonviolence. In *Transforming Conflict and Anger into Peace and Nonviolence: A Spiritual Direction*, Janet Malone offers solid spirituality and practical information. Malone's clear and precise language is evidenced in her insightful reflections on both conflict and anger:

> When we are chronically angry, we have great difficulty letting go, of the specific hurt at hand, but also of our victim identity. We reach a point at which we lose the essence of who we are apart from being a victim. To

let go of this acquired identity is scary because, without it, we would no longer know who we are.... Blaming and learned helplessness become a way of life. When we hold on to a hurt or a grudge for years and years a part of us dies: our self-esteem, our spontaneity, our laughter, our energy, our dreams.... Conflict nudges us out of complacency into chaos and disorder, the catalyst of new growth. Conflict is an occasion to deepen a given relationship...

This is the stuff of grace, of occasions for conversion. But, ah, the great mystery of the heart: how some move with the graces offered for conversion and how others stay stuck!

The hope always is that anger and conflict will surface the deepest possible healing – at least in the long run. Along the way there may be greater wounding and even despair. What draws me to *Transforming Conflict* is that it brings some of the more common analyses of anger and conflict into the depth and breadth of the mystery of love and faith – including Christ's call to love our enemies. It is an attempt to go beyond the safe margins to a place where there are no guarantees of easy success. If we live outside the normal, if we are willing to live on the margins and take risks of the heart, we inevitably encounter disturbing, painful realities – wounds we would not otherwise choose to confront. Malone notes, "Dialogue is a face-to-face sharing of the differences that have become issues between us … so we can come to some deep place of being and knowing our own and each other's stories … nurturing a relationship in constructive and nonviolent ways is more important than winning and being right." This holds true in the face of despair and even of separation.

Transforming Conflict is meant to challenge and to heal. It is a vital contribution to freeing up the energy needed to create a culture of nonviolence where we can pass on a new story to our children about the earth and about our enemies.

We are all wounded. Malone reflects on those critical incidents related to anger and conflict – the inevitable traumas of life and relationships: "Blessing leads to integration. After naming my hurt, and owning it in all its pain, blessing is a gradual move to integrate this experience.... I am who I am today, because of – not in spite of – that critical incident." It is never as much about success or failure or even mental and spiritual health as it is about the mysterious journey towards love – no matter where it leads. Christ invites us to become as mature in love as God is (Matt. 5:48). *Transforming Conflict* can assist us in the mysterious, life-long journey – a liberating journey towards respect, gentleness and, finally, joy.

Leonard Desroches
December 2006

PREFACE

This book is my invitation to you to let go of the violence that is often associated with conflict and anger and to transform their energies into growth and non-violence. It is a resource book for consultants, trainers, health-care professionals, counsellors, religious congregations and clergy that features a combination of theory and practice. Although written from a Christian perspective, its focus and scope are intended to be respectful of other faiths and spiritualities.

The book focuses on intrapersonal and interpersonal conflict and anger rather than their national or international aspects. The intrapersonal has received short shrift in the literature; this book intends to help restore the balance.

I set the context for intrapersonal and interpersonal conflict by looking at our "home" as the cosmic community – the organic, quantum and biocentric universe of which the Earth is a part. I then use the principles of the Earth Charter as the "house rules" to follow as we learn how to transform our intrapersonal and interpersonal conflict and anger energies.

I approach conflict and anger from the perspective of a spirituality of nonviolence. This is both a way of life and a methodology that helps keep us grounded when we are inundated with "quick and dirty" solutions for dealing with our conflict and anger.

I offer my own definitions and approaches to conflict, anger, violence, nonviolence, spirituality, communication, forgiveness and reconciliation based on the research, writing and teaching I have done and on the retreats and skills-training sessions I have facilitated over the years. I also include original figures and tables, and, in Appendix A, a personal anger assessment survey. I incorporate the research, writing and insights of other disciplines; however, I have, in fact, moved away from a number of established approaches.

I believe conflict and anger are normal, natural, necessary and even beneficial processes for our own and others' growth. A strong and substantive response to conflict and anger is one that combines good theory with nonviolent practices for dealing with their energies in constructive and life-giving ways. Learning to think and act in this new way is a lifelong pilgrimage of conversion that we make one step at a time. It is my hope that this book will help you deepen or begin that transforming journey.

PART I

COSMIC COMMUNITY CONTEXT

1

HOME

A community is never there for itself. It belongs to something greater... the universe.

Jean Vanier

Our New Story

Most of us have a very specific notion of home: the place where we were born and grew up with our family. But have you ever thought of Earth as your home, and the cosmos as your global community? Ecology (from the Greek *oikos*, meaning *home*) is the branch of biology that deals with the relationships among all living beings on Earth. From an ecological perspective, then, home is both our particular experience and the larger context of right relations with all life. Cosmic consciousness involves recognizing the deep sense of life, order and oneness in the universe. We have rights, but so do all other life forms; we therefore have no right to dominate, control or disturb the sacred web of life.

This is a new way of looking at the idea of home: a new story. The old story was built on the belief that a very small group of people counts and the rest do not; that through models of pyramids, hierarchies and dualisms, humans were dominant, entitled to abuse and misuse everything beneath them.

The new story is built on the belief that we are all kin and that each person and life form is intrinsically valuable, to be treated respectfully. We must learn to live interdependently, interconnectedly, reciprocally and mutually, acknowledging the rights and responsibilities of all.

The Earth is often described in terms of the female body. Ecofeminism, a specific area of study about the Earth, emphasizes the sacredness of all matter and connects women's bodies and Mother Earth. According to Hazel Henderson, "Ecofeminism resacralizes nature"[1] and, therefore, women. It counteracts the objectification of both the Earth and women's bodies, which results in raping, ravaging and plundering.

Western philosophy is steeped in hierarchical dualisms, that "either/or" worldview in which the first named is the subject, and the second is the object. The object is derivative, with no intrinsic essence or beauty. Out of dualism, we have learned that "objects are 'things' that others can change as they please with no consequences, while subjects both affect others and are affected by them."[2] Until we realize that our new story is about us all as subjects, then the physical as well as the psychological and spiritual raping will continue.

Ecospirituality, another aspect of ecology, recognizes the equality, mutuality, interconnectedness and interdependence of all creation. It is a lens through which we can see the whole Earth and all life forms as sacred, "as in earlier times, embodying the spirit and wonder of creation."[3] Ecospirituality challenges us to realize that setting the human community apart from the rest of creation results in violence and oppression, a timely reminder in this, UNESCO's International Decade for a Culture of Peace for the Children of the World (2001–2010).

Our evolving universe helps us put the new story of our home in perspective. Our observable universe is 12 to 15 billion years old. Cosmology helps us understand our biocentric, global community as part of an "organic unity where everything is related to everything else internally from the beginning."[4] At its beginnings, the universe "was concentrated in a singularity, maybe the size of a pinhead that was unimaginably hot and unimaginably dense."[5] In what has become known as the Big Bang, the compacted space of that singularity expanded very rapidly and then let loose. In the first three minutes, all sorts of physical changes took place, resulting in what we now know as subatomic particles and many galaxies, including the Milky Way. As things settled somewhat, the Milky Way, a medium-sized galaxy, and the sun, one of its spiral arms, were formed from atoms released by a nearby supernova. With the creation of the sun, some of its surrounding material formed into orbiting planets, one of which was Earth.

The evolution of our universe can be described as a cosmic dance of energy, movement and rhythm. This internal, co-creative process suggests "God as a participator in the creative process...responsible for ordering the world, not through direct action, but in providing various potentialities which the physical universe is then free to actualize."[6]

Another way to understand and appreciate our home is to look at Earth's periods of development. The Paleozoic era, 570 to 230 million years ago, was highlighted by the development of the first fishes, reptiles, amphibians and land plants. The Mesozoic era, 230 to 66 million years ago, was the age of dinosaurs, marine life, flying reptiles and evergreen trees. According to Mary Conrow Coelho, we have now come to the end of the Cenozoic era (66 million years ago to the present).[7] It was during this era, about 100,000 years ago, that humans as we know us today (*homo sapiens*) evolved out of Africa.

Now in the Ecozoic era, as named by leading ecotheologian Thomas Berry, we are beginning to recognize our subject-to-subject relationship with all life in our planet and cosmic community. According to Berry, "the great work" of this era is to establish ways of being and doing that view "the universe as a communion of subjects rather than a collection of objects."[8] We are starting to see home as an organic whole, "a living system which has its own intelligence."[9]

Peter Russell suggests we have moved through the genesis of the earth (geogenesis) and the genesis of all life (biogenesis), moving now to the Omega Point through the genesis of the mind, cosmic consciousness (or as Teilhard de Chardin called it, "noogenesis").[10]

The final aspect of the new story of home is the Gaia Theory (*Gaia* is Greek for *earth*). This theory, the work of two bioscientists, James Lovelock and Lynn Margulis, suggests that the Earth evolved at a time when the precise environmental conditions occurred for its survival and ours. The Gaia Theory has been instrumental in an emerging shift from a human-centred and male-dominated worldview to a holistic and universe-centred one. It has been a move from "attention on human and cultural affairs to the affairs of Planet Earth as a living system of interdependent species."[11]

Community

We are at a crossroads in the history and story of our home.

In Newton's deterministic world, all elements in the universe were viewed as stable, predictable, isolated and independent. Atoms were considered the building blocks of the universe, and the total universe equalled the sum of the individual atoms. Such a worldview emphasized an objective reality that we could name, analyze and control. Most of us were raised on this Newtonian worldview, which places great emphasis on equilibrium, stability and the status quo.

The new story of home has shifted from Newton's linear universe of atoms (a mechanistic worldview) to Einstein's universe of relativity and subatomic particles (an organic, biocentric worldview), the energy of which – quanta – forms an interrelated, interconnected and interdependent whole. What this means is that our home is a cosmic community of relationships. It is not made up of isolated building blocks as we were once taught, but rather of patterns of interrelating energy. Being in community means learning to see the deeper patterns of oneness behind the seeming disparities, and living in right relationships with all living beings.

First Nations people believe that we must live our lives in view of the future of the next seven generations. In Gaian terms, we are not the final goal of evolution. In fact, such misguided human-centred thinking has led us to the point at which our future as a species is at stake. We are beginning to realize the devastation our so-called human progress has wreaked on the earth. After centuries of living in our home as though it were a machine, there to serve only our excessive consumerism and human progress, we are seeing the insidious results. Our control over the nonhuman world has caused "the plundering of the earth's resources and disrupting the basic functioning of the life systems of the planet."[12]

Is the new story of Earth just a utopian dream? The hero of the classic book *The Little Prince* visited many planets, including Earth. His conclusion: "The earth is not just an ordinary planet."[13] Each of us is on a conversion journey toward right relations with Earth, but like the Little Prince's fox friend, we may need to be tamed.

To be tamed is to establish ties, to be interconnected and interdependent. Our challenge and responsibility in the Ecozoic Age is remembering his admonition: "What you have tamed you become responsible for."[14] Of course, this taming is reciprocal. In establishing ties in our biocentric universe, I tame and am tamed; I am responsible for ensuring the future of my home (to seven generations) and the Earth is responsible for me. Such is the nature of our cosmic community; such is the nature of unconditional, agapic love.

In C.S. Lewis' *The Four Loves*, he speaks of four kinds of love: *philia/storge*, *amitia*, *eros* and *agape* (Greek for unconditional love). He sees the first three – love of family, friends and lovers, respectively – as varieties of conditional love. Agapic love, by contrast, is unconditional: the seemingly impossible love Jesus modelled. Agapic love touches us at the core of our beings, where we are challenged to the depths of conversion.

Agapic love is gift-love, and is a conversion journey away from our preoccupying need-love and immediate gratification. Through gift-love, we can see the big picture and put life in a context of awe and gratitude. "Gift love…is wholly disinterested and desires what is simply best for the beloved…,"[15] says Lewis. It is what makes our planet our home, and our cosmos, community. To move together for the common good of all, we strive to change our conditional love into agapic love as we transform our conflict and anger energies.

Agapic love is a daily living out of St. Paul's description of gift-love (1 Corinthians 13:4-8). Love is patient, kind, rejoices with the truth, bears all things, believes, hopes, dreams, endures. Love is not jealous, does not brag, is not arrogant. Love never fails. This, then, is our daily challenge for forming community. It is our unconditional willing of good for others, especially our enemies. It is our equal regard for the well-being of all others, to the point of our willingness to sacrifice ourselves for their sake. In the words of Timothy Jackson, "Agape is willing the good of the whole person as well as the wider community."[16]

As we will see, unconditional love becomes the essence of learning how to love our enemy in the heat of conflict and anger; how to let go of fears that engender hate, violence and oppression. Such agapic love is essential for any fullness of life for ourselves and our global community, when indiscriminate and ongoing violence threatens.

Earth Charter

I still remember my excitement when I read in *The Aquarian Conspiracy* about the notion of critical mass: the change in consciousness that happens when a new idea gradually grows from being the dream of one or two to having a life of its own, when enough disparate people are talking about the same thing. I suggest that this is what is happening today as we move from our old story to our new story. We see science, religion, psychology, sociology, mathematics, astrology, astronomy, ecology and cosmology all converging into a critical mass, saying the same thing.

Are you ready to become part of the critical mass telling our new story? Do not be discouraged because our old story is in the marrow of our bones. As Robert M. Augros and George N. Stanciu say in their book *The New Story of Science: Mind and the Universe,* "The Old Story is not functioning properly and we have not learned the New Story.... A worldview is so fundamental that it cannot be changed quickly or easily – even if there is compelling evidence for a change. Instead, there is always the tendency to force the new knowledge into the old view."[17]

Read the Earth Charter (www.earthcharter.org/files/charter/charter.pdf) for your own set of house rules, to help you learn the new story. This charter, approved by the United Nations World Commission on Environment and Development in March 2000, is the result of seven UN summit conferences in the 1990s, including the 1992 Rio de Janeiro conference, when UN members began work on it.

A declaration of fundamental principles (house rules) for building a just, sustainable and peaceful global society in the 21st century, the charter is based on contemporary science, philosophy and the world's religions. It is a framework for living together in a new sense of global interdependence and shared responsibility. The Earth Charter's inclusive ethical vision recognizes that environmental protection, the rights of all life forms, nonviolence and peace are interdependent and indivisible. It contains several principles, notably,

> *respect and care for the community of life;

> *ecological integrity;

> *social and economic justice; and

> *democracy, nonviolence and peace.

The Earth Charter Preamble reiterates our part in the community of life:

> We stand at a critical moment in Earth's history, a time when humanity must choose its future. As the world becomes increasingly interdependent and fragile, the future at once holds great peril and great promise.

To move forward we must recognize that in the midst of a magnificent diversity of cultures and life forms we are one human family and one Earth community with a common destiny.... Humanity is part of a vast evolving universe.... The spirit of human solidarity and kinship with all life is strengthened when we live with reverence for the mystery of being, gratitude for the gift of life, and humility regarding the human place in nature....

PART I: REFLECTION AND DISCUSSION STARTERS

1. What comforts you in the new story about our home? What challenges you?

2. Do you agree that we need a cosmic community context for our discussion of conflict and anger? Why or why not?

3. In what ways does agapic love highlight who you are at your best?

4. Do the "house rules" of the Earth Charter need to be part of your life? Why or why not?

PART II

A SPIRITUALITY OF NONVIOLENCE

2

VIOLENCE TO NONVIOLENCE

*Violence becomes the stock in trade of a
patriarchal system.*

Joan Chittister

You probably remember vividly where you were and what you were doing when
you learned of the terrorist attacks on September 11, 2001. I was participating in
an annual staff meeting, where we were looking at how we could be more open,
less hierarchical and more focused on sharing rather than abusing power.

In the wake of the attacks, when national and international threats for retribution
were high in many cities and countries, Women for Peace/Artisanes de la Paix – a
group of women of various faiths and cultures living in Ottawa, Canada – met to
look at how we might respond nonviolently. We knew at a deep level of our beings that our efforts to promote nonviolence – peace rather than revenge – would
affect the whole cosmic community in some way, beginning with our own.

Believing that peace and nonviolence can be learned from those who walk their
talk, we wrote a vision statement.

Women for Peace/Les Artisanes de la Paix

We are women
of many cultures, many faiths,
coming together as sisters,
to witness to our common values of peace, love and nonviolence,
for the sake of our children,
our families, our earth.

The green we wear
symbolizes our longing for peace,
our hope for nonviolent resolution
of conflicts, and our valuing
of all life in creation.

Each Wednesday, from 12:15 to 12:45 p.m., we would pray silently for peace on Parliament Hill, around the Eternal Flame, holding the banner carrying our name and wearing our green scarves of hope for a less violent world.

Occasionally, a politician would stop and ask what we were doing, or others passing by might pick up one of our vision statement cards or join our group and pray with us. Even those who were hesitant to stand with us might give us the thumbs-up sign, tacitly approving of our peace action. Sometimes a man might join us in solidarity and prayer, which was heartening, since it is all of us together who will change our old story to the new one.

I cannot say what our nonviolent prayerful stance did in concrete terms, week after week, through rain and shine. Yet I have no doubt that, in the cosmic community where we are all part of the web of life, hearts were changed.

The Term *Nonviolence*

Before we explore the spirituality of nonviolence, let us examine the word *nonviolence* itself. There is no doubt that it is a problematic word for many, including me. About ten years ago, I began to seek alternative names for it. I wanted a more positive, challenging and uplifting term.

Nonviolence is the direct translation of the Sanskrit word *ahimsa*, which is taken from some of the ancient Hindu texts. It means "non-harm" or "inoffensiveness" and is based on the Hindu belief in the universal oneness of all created beings. Gandhi wrote, "*Ahimsa* means love in the sense of St. Paul and much more." Gandhi professed to see profound similarities between the *Bhagavad-Gita* and the Sermon on the Mount.[1] To describe *ahimsa,* he coined the term *satyagraha,* translated as "soul force" or "power of truth."

The four prophets of nonviolence featured in Chapter 3 use different terms for nonviolence: Gandhi, *ahimsa* and *satyagraha*; Dorothy Day, *pacifism*; Etty Hillesum, *love of the enemy*; Leonard Desroches, *dunamis*.

When Leonard Desroches is asked about the word *nonviolence*, he suggests that the time may not be ripe for another term. Until we can move away from the cycle of violence to a lived reality of nonviolence, this may be the best term to express where we are. In his book *Allow the Water*, Desroches elaborates, "I believe that 'non'-violence – the lack of violence – reflects where we are historically, attempting to go from violence to 'non'-violence…. We need to deepen our understanding of how the real alternative to the force of fear, greed, hatred and destruction is not merely lack of violence but the very real force of love."[2]

Promise of Paradox

Our new story of home is one in which we live in the tension of the both/and as we move away from an either/or stance of control and security: either good or bad, either light or dark, either violence or nonviolence. Hence the paradox. In looking at nonviolence, we must embrace our violence; we can only know the one in the context of the other. This journey to nonviolence is primarily a pilgrimage of the heart. We look at nature and see violence in other life forms – the fight-or-flight violence related to survival and procreation. In our evolution, we humans have developed a self-reflective kind of consciousness in which we can think about and change what we know, see and do. This is our contribution to all life. In moving to a spirituality of nonviolence we must be clear about what violence looks like and sounds like in our daily lives. Only when we can reflect on this violence and embrace it as part of us can we transform its energies to nonviolence.

What is violence for you? The more I acknowledge the various and subtle forms of violence in my own life, the more I see its pervasiveness – how my violent acts of word, deed and omission beget other acts of violence, against myself but also against others. Violence takes myriad forms: a brilliant but sarcastic remark here, a push or shove of someone or something there. These acts grow like a cancer, spreading to all aspects of my life. Of course, each of us can recognize violence in others more readily than in ourselves; we may also be ready to judge others on their acts while denying or rationalizing our own. Such is the insidious nature of violence.

Psychological and spiritual violence was rarely acknowledged in my family, church and society when I was growing up. Only physical violence was "real," because there was visible proof. We are only beginning to connect people's scars to psychological and spiritual violence as they come forward with their stories, years and years later.

We may believe that physical violence counts only when it affects humans, since in our old story we were taught that humans are the apex of creation and the masters and dominators of all. We may not understand from a biocentric universe perspective that all life forms have their own unique intelligence and are affected by violence.

War: Organized Violence

Think of the number of wars being fought right now. War, whose goal is to eliminate the enemy, is the most obvious form of organized violence approved by the state (in most cases) and perpetrated by humans. I have not experienced the violence and ravages of war, yet more and more I am able to see that the seeds of such extreme violence are everywhere, starting with me.

We are familiar with the graphic images of the physical violence of war: torn limbs, shattered bodies, destruction and death. But we are less aware of the psychological and spiritual violence of war. A case in point is what is now known as post-traumatic stress syndrome, with its attendant physical, psychological and spiritual effects on people who have been in very violent and stressful situations, such as war. These complex reactions used to be attributed to cowardice and lack of stamina; today, we know better. I believe my own father suffered from an undiagnosed case of post-traumatic stress syndrome. Part of the Normandy invasion during the Second World War, he watched many of his fellow sailors die. His waking nightmare had profound effects on our entire family.

Violence Defined

Aggression, defined as an unprovoked attack, warlike act or bold hostility, comprises many of the same actions as violence. The word *violence* most often refers to physical force so as to injure. Hocker and Wilmot note, "Many conflict interactions go beyond threats and verbal aggression and result in physical violence."[3]

Recalling the house rules of our new story of home, I suggest that violence is all inclusive: the physical, psychological, spiritual abuse of all life forms.

Expanding the parameters of violence beyond physical violence is an important step forward in raising our awareness. Conflict resolution expert Vern Neufeld Redekop's definition of violence includes all types of violence (although only towards humans). He states that violence can take various forms but "it is intended to hurt, harm, damage, destroy or to otherwise dis-empower a person. It is an intrusion on the dignity of another"; it "takes away from the well-being of someone…, causes death, physical injury or psychological damage, prompts negative emotion or results in a wounded spirit."[4]

Theologian Walter Wink also details the many aspects of violence in his exploration of power: violence, domination and the myth of redemptive violence; human violence and the creation myths; and violence and religion. He notes, "Human beings are created from the blood of a murdered god. Our very origin is violence … the ritual practice of violence is at the very heart of public life."[5] He links violence and today's economic injustice and oppression, saying, "A society with an unfair distribution of goods requires violence."[6]

Nature vs. Nurture

Do you have stereotypes about people and violence, related to personality, age, gender or race? Is violence innate or learned? Are both women and men naturally aggressive and violent? Answering these questions helps us look at our own violence, even the violence we may still deny is part of us.

Today, we are beginning to see more clearly that violence is learned; enactments of violence are socially constructed. "Violence and aggression are not hereditary. No one is born violent…. With direct and indirect influence…one may be conditioned and accept violence as a way of life,"[7] says Carmen Germaine Warner.

What is the role of the mass media in sowing a desire for violence? With a steady diet of both blatant and "entertaining" violence from media sources, our tolerance increases; we read more newspaper and magazine articles and watch more movies and TV shows that feature violence. Even our newscasts portray violence in such a way that it doesn't seem real anymore.

Cycle of Violence

Violence breeds violence. That is why peace is
rooted in prayer, in grace.

Matthew Kelty

Coming to grips with my own violence has helped me see its ebb and flow, its phases that recur unless I consciously work to stop the cycle.

The *first phase*, the build-up of tension, stems from the chronic and cumulative pent-up energies of our intrapersonal and interpersonal relationships that have not been processed.

The *second phase*, the outburst of explosive behaviour, is the straw that breaks the camel's back. A triggering event, which usually has little or nothing to do with the present conflict and anger, leads to violence in word or action or both. Although this phase may not last very long, it is the heart of the cycle of violence. It is the supposed cathartic release of resentments that have not been dealt with.

The *third phase*, with its promises that it will never happen again, becomes the "kiss and make up" phase. Here the abuser, with a momentary respite from tension, feels guilty and repents the violence and abuse. However, because the underlying issues have not been dealt with, there will be a next time, and the cycle of violence continues.

In the cycle of violence, a mutual dependence, even a co-dependence, is created. For example, women blame themselves for the violence, and with lowered self-esteem stay in abusive and violent relationships. This type of violence is about control and power in the form of ongoing physical, psychological and spiritual abuse. Known as the battered wife syndrome, it can be found in other intimate relationships as well.

We receive mixed messages about violence. Our social, political and ecclesial systems decry the increase in violence and yet teach us to be competitive, aggressive, successful, highly individualistic and self-reliant.

Many sports, even for children, encourage aggression, and I see all competition as violent. Toys and videogames invite players to play out violent scenarios. Police officers and peace keepers are known to use violent means at times to subdue others.

Denial of Death

When we see another person not as a subject but only as an object for our use, abuse and misuse to help extend our comfort and life, then we may be denying death, particularly our own.

Rather than focusing on getting ahead and being successful, we can work on developing and nurturing the contemplative side of ourselves, with emphasis on a better balance between being and doing.

Sports journalist Mitch Albom learned about living and dying when he reconnected with his professor Morrie Schwartz just at the time when Schwartz was dying from ALS (amyotrophic lateral sclerosis). Albom later wrote about the essence of their conversations on life and death in a powerful little book, *Tuesdays with Morrie*. Schwartz shared with Albom his love of life and acceptance of death, seeing the interdependence between the two. "Once you learn how to die, you learn how to live. When you realize you are going to die, you see everything differently."[8]

Ernest Becker reiterates this fear and denial in his groundbreaking work, *The Denial of Death*. "Since the terror of death is so overwhelming, we try to keep it unconscious…to pretend that the world is manageable."[9]

When we safeguard the preciousness of our life at the expense of other lives, then we live with a "power over" worldview and its inherent violence. When we can accept diminishment and death as part of the normal life cycle, then "awareness of the shortness of time renders life more precious."[10]

Nonviolence

Nonviolence tests our patience, our power to love.

Cesar Chavez

Conscientization

My own journey into nonviolence stems from two separate but interconnected incidents. In the 1980s, when I had the opportunity to do extended research, I chose the topic of conflict and anger in religious organizations. As a member of one such organization, I saw considerable violence. These organizations emphasized that "holy" and "praying" people did not experience conflict and anger, which led to strenuous denials of both. Yet the effects of suppressed conflict and anger were obvious: the silent treatment, sabotaging, depression and addiction.

Shortly after completing my research, I attended an international meeting of my religious organization. While exploring objectives for the next mandate, someone suggested nonviolence. When one person announced to the whole assembly that we did not need to look at violence because of our religious commitment, the light went on for me. I was part of an organization in denial about its violence. It was then that I was able to use the word *violent* to describe many of the unhealthy behaviours I had witnessed over the years.

A Brief History of Nonviolence

Nonviolence is not the latest "success" strategy of modern gurus. It is not a quick fix. Nonviolence is a philosophy, a tactic, a strategy, a spirituality, a way of life that goes back to the *Tao Te Ching,* the *Bhagavad-Gita* and the *Upanishads,* the *Talmud,* the *Koran* and the Hebrew and Christian scriptures. Each of these sacred texts describes the essence of nonviolence in similar terms: sustaining attack and violence, and protecting oneself assertively but without retaliatory violence. It is Jesus' Third Way: loving one's enemy. The similarities among some of the world's oldest religions and philosophies regarding nonviolence are remarkable.

Jainism, considered older than Hinduism and Buddhism, is a religion based on nonviolence. Its members, called ascetics, follow a very strict way of life, espousing absolute nonviolence as the way to attain liberation or *moksa*. Jainism "accepts and advocates nonviolence as the highest ideal of life."[11] The ascetics take vows, including those of truthfulness, sexual continency, non-possession and nonviolence.

Hinduism originated in India. Gandhi, perhaps its most famous proponent, was known for his nonviolent actions and approach. He espoused the essence of the Gita, which teaches its followers to live deliberately and to act in harmony with the real self.

The Chinese learned nonviolence from the teachings of Lao Tzu (Taoism) and Confucius (Confucianism), as found in the *Tao Te Ching* and the *Way of Chuang Tzu*. The *Tao* is described as the way and the ultimate indefinable reality.

Buddhism, the dominant spirituality of most parts of Asia, Indochina and Japan, is based on the Buddha's focus on enlightenment, the Four Noble truths, and the Eightfold Path of self-development. The first principle of the Buddha is commitment to nonviolence. Hatred does not cease by hatred; only love can overcome hatred.

Jewish Talmudic sources highlight nonviolence as a unique way of responding to conflict. "The doctrine of nonviolence affirms that our humanity unites us more that our conflicts divide us."[12]

For many, Jesus is the model par excellence of nonviolence. His Sermon on the Mount challenges not only not to harm our enemy, but to love our enemy. Based on Jesus' faith, love and forgiveness, his followers lived "the Way," the Christian message.

This message has proven difficult for Christians to live: from the Roman emperor Constantine hunting out and persecuting Christians, then later (as a Christian) persecuting and conquering other groups and nations through force, nonviolence as part of Christianity was now gone. Armed force by the state was the norm.

Lawrence S. Apsey explains, "Had he been sensitive to the tenderness of the divine love, Constantine would have understood his vision to mean that he should conquer by love, courage and self-sacrifice."[13]

Since the fourth century, Christianity has advocated nonviolence in theory. In practice, however, the example of Constantine, rather than that of Christ, has continued in varying forms and degrees, especially in the Just War teaching.[14] War, as organized violence, is never just and never justified.

Organizational Misuse

Nonviolence is not a garment
to be put on and off at will.
Its seat is in the heart and it must be
an inseparable part of our being.

Gandhi

Religion and Spirituality

Many people see religion and spirituality as synonymous. Others distinguish between the two as the letter of the law (religion) and the spirit of the law (spirituality). "Religion is basically concerned with externals, with rites, dogmas, special buildings, castes of clergy and all the rest,"[15] says Tom Harpur. The formal religion that we know today is about 5,000 years old, whereas spirituality, rooted in our evolutionary story, is about 600,000 years old.[16]

The word *religion*, which comes from the Latin *religare*, to connect, suggests a uniting of all aspects of our lives. However, in many of our present-day religions that emphasize sin and salvation, the *via negativa* and power in the hands of authority, religion has become the control of the many by the few, all in God's name. Theology, the formal study of God, has become linked to formal religion and supremacy: our God, not yours; our religion, not yours. The various denominations purport to have the "real" God, to the point of controlling God with ultimatums such as, "Outside the church, there is no salvation."[17] John Shelby Spong, Anglican Bishop of Newark, New Jersey, gave a talk in England in 2003 during which he spoke at length about religion and its historic divisiveness. He noted, "Religion is one of the most divisive forces in the world today. It has always been."

Spong suggested that religion is a carry-over from the tribal prejudices and stereotypes of our forebears, a way to feel superior over other tribes and mask our real feelings of inferiority and fear. In bravado, tribes developed principles, values and beliefs based on notions of "superior to," "better than," "ours, the one true faith," and "ours, the one true God."

Patriarchy denotes head of the household and, by extension, the church. Religion, with its attendant patriarchy and control over male lineage, ensures the dominance of the male lineage. Religion evolved as part of the Agricultural Revolution, when formal religion became a way for landowners to try and gain supremacy over God. "Today, we have outlived that agricultural phase of our evolutionary development, and so quite appropriately, thousands of people are leaving religion aside, no longer feeling the need for it. Formal religion is being replaced with spirituality, the human search for meaning."[18]

Things spiritual (from the Latin *spirare*: to breathe) are of the essence of life. We were born spiritual beings, so spirituality is integral and essential to our conversion, growth and transformation. "Spirituality concerns an ancient and primal search for meaning that is as old as humanity itself and…belongs – as an inherent energy – to the evolutionary unfolding of creation itself," explains Diarmuid O'Murchu, a priest and social psychologist.[19] Spirituality is that luminous membrane connecting the human and the divine.

We meet people of many religious faiths or of no faith who have a rich spiritual life that is truly inspiring. Their spirituality is nurtured by a deep prayer life and a commitment to love. Spiritual people trust the sacred space of all of creation and look for the poetry as well as the prose in life. They are able to live with incompleteness and do not need to have all their questions answered. They see no dichotomy between the sacred and the profane.

Spirituality is about integrating all in one's life. As theologian Sandra Schneiders suggests, "It represents…a profound and authentic desire…for wholeness in the midst of fragmentation, community in the face of isolation and loneliness for liberating transcendence, for meaning in life, for values that endure."[20]

A spirituality of nonviolence is essential in dealing with conflict and anger. It crosses all religions and faiths; it is a way of life bigger than one religion, emerging from the spirit and Spirit of all life as equal, sacred, fragile and interconnected. It involves a deep prayer life, a recognition of our own powerlessness and an acceptance of God as the source and force of spiritual power. This power gives us the courage to denounce violence, starting with the violence within us, so we can announce the nonviolence of the Good News of the reign of God.

Living a spirituality of nonviolence is not just a decision; it is, first and foremost, a gift and a grace. It requires a conversion to a way of life that leads to nonviolent actions and strategies for raising consciousness and eventually transforming situations and lives. It is an ever-moving, ever-changing energy that unfolds and blossoms. If it is not engaged in all aspects of our life, it becomes static and stale.

Ongoing daily conversion is key to the spirituality of nonviolence. The goal is always the transformation of both sides, not the victory of one over the other. Grounded in our new story, it leads to each side respecting the other, rather than dominating through violence.

3

FOUR PROPHETS OF NONVIOLENCE

A prophet is an oddity –
a scandal or a nuisance or a bore or an outrage,
according to the degree
in which he/she interferes
with the normal order of things.

Rosemary Haughton

The Prophet

When learning how to develop a spirituality of nonviolence, it helps to have as models people who have lived or are living this way of life.

Living out the prophetic call requires a deep prayer life. Nobody sets out to be a prophet. Rather, it is a dynamic call-response from God that encompasses the individual's personality, intelligence, heart and spirit. Because prophets must be able to stand alone, to speak alone when others disapprove or are too afraid to upset the status quo, they must be able to draw on a deep well of faith, trust and hope, even when they are not sure of the next steps, or when they face criticism, marginalization, arrest, jail and even death.

The gift of prophecy is a conversion that stretches over a lifetime.

In theologian Walter Brueggemann's classic book, *The Prophetic Imagination,* he speaks of a prophetic ministry as one involving nourishing, nurturing and evolving a way of being and doing that is an alternative to the dominant ethos. The prophet's dual role is both critical and energizing. He explains, "It is precisely the prophet who speaks against…and who can energize toward futures that are genuinely new and not derived…to bring to expression the new realities against the more visible ones of the old order."[1]

Elsewhere, I have called this role one of both denunciation and annunciation.[2] The prophet denounces what is violent, oppressive and unjust in a relationship or group in order to announce the reign of God as characterized by love, interdependence, mutuality, reciprocity and justice. Denunciation is not mere negativity, carping and grousing. Rather, it gives rise to the annunciation of true life.

"The characteristic way of a prophet…is that of poetry. Indeed, poetic imagination is the last way left in which to challenge and conflict the dominant reality," says Brueggemann.[3] The prophet is a loving critic and a critical lover whose vision of an alternative reality is grounded and supported in a life of prayer, simplicity, silence and solitude. As a risk-taker and challenger, the prophet calls others forth to right relationships in the "new" reign of God, all in the name of justice and agapic love, but is ready to go it alone when others cannot, or will not, join in community for a better world. For Rosemary Haughton, "The test of the true prophet, that she/he has been transformed, converted, reconciled, sent – not drunk with his/her own cleverness but with the spirit – is that the prophetic word is a 'converting word.' The power the prophet shows is solely a power to provoke faith, to convert…the agent of transformation."[4]

Establishing healthy boundaries is essential in times of loneliness and fearfulness, when there is the temptation to seek comfort from the familiar. Through the discipline of daily time in prayer with Jesus in the wilderness, the prophet finds the courage to span the gap between what is and what must be.

The prophet learns over time to live a life of isolation and marginalization and to endure the disrespect and criticism of others. The prophet learns to be a good gardener, planting the seeds of nonviolence, love and justice for self and others. As a result of prayer, groundedness, faith, love and hope, the seeds eventually blossom in good soil and yield much fruit. Many prophets do not see the dream realized; instead, others reap the harvest.

This prophetic call demands changes in the prophet as well, bringing about a deeper self-knowledge. The false self, with its hubris, impatience and lack of tolerance is transformed into a more centred, focused, tolerant person who realizes that she or he has no power (political, social or religious) other than the power and love of God. Even when nothing tangible happens in the world as a result of the prophet's actions, such transformation in a quantum universe affects all life for future generations.

Many prophets of nonviolence have made a commitment to both the theory and practice of the spirituality of nonviolence: Francis of Assisi, Catherine of Siena, Oscar Romero, Jean Donovan, Thomas Gumbleton, Walter Wink, Thomas Merton, Daniel Berrigan, Phil Berrigan and Elizabeth MacAlister, Martin Luther King, Desmond Tutu, Nelson Mandela, Rosa Parks, Daw Aung San Suu Kyi, Hildegard Goss-Mayr, Eileen Egan and Evelyn Jegen, to name just a few.[5]

As you read about the four modern prophets below – Gandhi, Dorothy Day, Etty Hillesum and Leonard Desroches – think about how their lives enflesh a spirituality of nonviolence.

Gandhi (1869–1948)

Born in 1869 in Portbandar, near Bombay, Mohandas K. Gandhi was a shy, awkward child whose early school years were uneventful. In an arranged marriage to Kasturbai (both were 13 years old), he says, "I lost no time in assuming the authority of a husband…. Kasturbai could go nowhere without my permission."[6]

At 19, Gandhi went to study law in London. Anxious to fit in, he adopted English food and dress customs. After being called to the bar in 1891, he returned to India and began working in a law firm. The law firm decided to send him to work in their office in Pretoria for a year, which turned into 21 years. His life from then on can be divided into two parts: his 21 years working for justice for his own people in South Africa (1893–1914), and his remaining years in India (1915–1948) working for justice for his people with the British government, including eliminating the salt tax, removing the stigmas of the untouchables caste, building a united India and seeking self-government. To prevent the division of India, Gandhi invited Muslims to Hindu prayers. On January 25, 1948, he was shot to death by a fellow Hindu who disapproved of such actions.

Two significant events began Gandhi's conversion to nonviolence. First, he defended a client in court but lost the case because he did not play by the rules of the hierarchical game. This incident had a profound impact on Gandhi because, although he was still not sure what he wanted to do with his life, it became clear what he did not want to do – that is, be involved in "petty intrigue, palace pomp, subservience and snobbery."[7]

Second, en route to his new job, a white man on the train demanded that Gandhi go to the coloured section, despite his being dressed as an educated Englishman. Insisting he had paid for his ticket, Gandhi refused and was eventually thrown off the train. This experience of colour prejudice set him on the journey to discover how to deal with such violence. Both in South Africa and India, he worked tirelessly for the rights of others through *satyagraha*.

Satyagraha requires ongoing nonviolent interaction between the two parties, with a view to eventually transforming the differences. *Satyagraha* is the "literal holding on to the truth, thus, truth-force or soul-force."[8] It is never physical force; a *satyagrahi* does not inflict pain on the other. "Nonviolence or soul-force...does not need physical aids for its propagation or effect. It transcends time and space.... The acid test of nonviolence is that one thinks, speaks and acts nonviolently, even when there is the gravest provocation to be violent."[9]

Conversion is gradual and, at times, imperceptible. In Gandhi's conversion, he became a more devout Hindu but also lived Christ's Sermon on the Mount, particularly loving his enemy. According to Leonard Desroches, "Beyond the strategies, Gandhi himself made clear the part that Christ – especially the Sermon on the Mount – played in his exploration of and his conversion to nonviolence."[10]

A Karma yogi, Gandhi meditated on the *Bhagavad Gita*, but, on the suggestion of a British salesman when he was in London, began reading the Hebrew and Christian scriptures as well. When he read the Beatitudes, he noted, "The Sermon on the Mount went straight to my heart."[11] It informed and enhanced his study and reflection of the *Gita*, from which came his spirituality and practice of nonviolence.

Gandhi's nonviolence did not come naturally. "He had a violent nature and his subsequent mahatama calm was the product of long training in temperament control. He did not easily become an even-minded desireless yogi," reports Louis Fischer, author of *Gandhi: His Life and Message for the World*. [12]

During his lifelong journey to nonviolence, Gandhi prepared his heart with prayer and meditation to meet nonviolently the injustice and oppression he encountered in South Africa and India. He invited the many people who followed him to do the same.

As he pondered the aspects of selflessness, lack of jealousy, forgiveness and contentedness in the *Gita*, Gandhi chose the word *desirelessness* to characterize them, "to act while renouncing interest in the fruits of action."[13] Over time, he modelled the inner peace and poise necessary to remain nonviolent in the midst of violence and oppression by conducting himself morally, not resisting arrest, submitting to police flogging, spending close to six years in jail and not taking advantage of his opponents. When all else failed in face-to-face meetings with both the South African and British governments, he fasted. He did so both for his own conversion to deeper and deeper truth, and for those choosing power over the people whose causes he championed.

Through love of enemy, prayer, fasting, simplicity of life, work toward self-support with a simple diet and sustaining occupation (his loin cloth and the spinning wheel became the metaphor of India's self-sufficiency), he became more focused and grounded as a *satyagrahi*.

Gandhi was convinced that nonviolence as a method was not enough. Walter Wink suggests that Gandhi developed it "into a movement complete with strategies and tactics."[14] The methods and means for particular nonviolent actions follow from scrupulous preparation, fasting and strategizing.

When asked whether he was a Christian, Gandhi boldly stated that he embraced Christ and, in some ways, was Christian, Hindu, Muslim and Jew. In the words of Eileen Egan, "While he relied on the age-old wisdom of India and its ancient law of self-sacrifice and *ahimsa*, Gandhi incorporated the wisdom of Christianity... [stating] 'I simply follow in the steps of a great teacher.'"[15]

Dorothy Day (1898–1980)

Born in 1898 in the midwest United States, Dorothy Day grew up in a family with Episcopalian roots. By her own admission, the family was neither religious nor churchgoing. An avid and thoughtful reader, she attended the University of Illinois for two years, where she socialized with students who were both writers and thinkers. In many conversations, particularly with her anarchist friends, she analyzed justice problems, offering definitive answers.

Lively, attractive and very aware of her sexuality, Day had a number of love affairs. She had an abortion in an effort to keep one of her lovers, realizing her pregnancy would jeopardize their relationship. Despite her active social life, however, she experienced deep loneliness. This loneliness was to be with her throughout her life, but it was a loneliness that she transformed over time into a lifelong commitment to the down and out.

In 1916, after she finished university, she moved to New York with her family. She lived very simply, working as a journalist like other members of her family.

Covering protests, she was appalled by what she saw: the homeless, the hungry, the unemployed. Later in life, when she protested herself, she was jailed for 30 days in a workhouse prison. In jail, she went on a ten-day hunger strike after she witnessed the plight of women prisoners and how violently they were treated.

During the First World War, Day nursed the sick. She also continued writing about the necessity of nonviolence, what she called pacifism, even encouraging conscientious objectors to burn their draft cards. She felt she was "pacifist in my views, pacifist in what I considered an imperialist war, though not pacifist as a revolutionist."[16] By her own admission, after some fifteen years of writing about pacifism, "we were just beginning to realize what it meant."[17] During this time, she was living with Forster Batterham. He was not in favour of marriage, so Day was content with being his partner. When she told him she was pregnant, their relationship changed. Day also became more reflective about how she was living her life. She decided to raise her daughter, Tamar, Catholic, so she would be grounded in God from the very beginning, something Day herself did not have but had always desired.

Raising Tamar, Day settled in to what she describes as one of the most peaceful periods of her life. She began to read the Psalms and the Sermon on the Mount, and eventually began to pray daily. For Day, "The Sermon on the Mount answered all the questions as to how to love God and one's brother [and sister]."[18]

In 1927, Day finally felt ready to become a Catholic herself. After instruction, she received the sacraments of conditional baptism (having already been baptized in the Episcopalian church), penance and eucharist. Her "dark night of the soul" lifted somewhat with her confirmation. Reflecting on this time, Day said, "I never regretted for one minute the step which I had taken in becoming a Catholic.... I loved the Church in Christ made visible."[19]

Peter Maurin came into Day's life around this time. A French peasant, an intellectual and a displaced person, Maurin had a passion for the poor person's ability to be self-sustaining. Day eventually called this man, some 20 years her senior, "the poor man of his day ... a Saint Francis of modern times."[20]

Day and Maurin, each dreaming of a better world, had many kitchen table discussions on this subject. He had a plethora of knowledge and wisdom about how to alleviate the plight of the poor and remake society with his "green house" revolution, complete with living simply on the land, building community with houses of hospitality, and places of training, "agronoma" universities. In her book *On Pilgrimage,* Dorothy referred to this system as the economics of distribution, in which the economic system is decentralized, encouraging the independent initiative of individuals.

Now that she was in her 30s, the season for her life work was beginning. In 1933, Day and Maurin teamed up, using the remarkable gifts of each, to begin the Catholic Worker Movement. The pillars of the movement were need for community; love expressed in works of mercy; commitment to eliminating racism, classism and war; and support of conscientious objectors. What began with one house of hospitality, where volunteers could come and go, and where the focus was working with the homeless, became a nationwide and, eventually, a worldwide movement.

Integral to the Catholic Worker Movement was its pacifist newspaper, *The Catholic Worker,* begun in May 1933 with Day as editor and an initial distribution of 2500 copies.

Day's gospel message of nonviolence was evident in the paper, and over time, she became fearless in announcing it. According to Eileen Egan, "It was Dorothy who proclaimed the message of gospel nonviolence or pacifism as she boldly announced it in the paper and the acts of witness that came to be characteristic of the movement,... the movement's gospel idealism."[21]

At the outbreak of the Second World War, some workers refused to distribute the *Catholic Worker* because of its pacifist stance. Day issued a statement, later known as her encyclical letter, that any Catholic Worker house refusing to distribute the paper should separate itself from the movement. Indeed, at this point, with her open encouragement of conscientious objectors, she "was considered so dangerous that in 1941 she was put on a US government list to consider for custodial detention in the event of a national emergency."[22]

With her abhorrence of any type of injustice and her talent for both speaking and writing, Day spent her life addressing injustices through pacifism, making it clear that pacifism was not passivism. Rather, it was a way of life, a spirituality built on prayer, solitude, fasting and simplicity. She spoke out fearlessly against the Just War theory and the use of force promoted by the government and the church.

In her later years, Day was involved in the houses of hospitality and in writing, speaking, protesting, fasting and going to jail. With her pacifism and what evolved as her discipleship of peace, Day's passion was that of "the followers of Jesus…grounded in a love that demanded simplicity of life, closeness to the poor and willingness to protest against the nation-state even at the cost of imprisonment."[23]

In 1963, during Vatican II, when the cardinals were working on the text for the encyclical *Peace on Earth* (*Pacem in Terris*), she was one of nineteen women who fasted and prayed that the cardinals would be enlightened to unequivocally condemn nuclear warfare and that the church would finally put an end to Constantine's legacy of "justified war." She also went to Rome to influence the cardinals' text for *The Church in the Modern World* (*Gaudium et Spes*), so that they would "include nonviolence as an essential element in living the gospel."[24]

Day died peacefully at age 82 in 1980 (Maurin had died several years earlier). She would say often, "All is grace," and her life was certainly grace-filled in her roles of mother, mother-in-law and grandmother. She had reached a point at which there was no distinction between what she believed, what she wrote and how she lived. "Love is the measure by which we shall be judged" is the first line of *On Pilgrimage*. Throughout her lifelong conversion to nonviolence, she lived a "love that must be tried, tested and proved…. True love must be delicate and kind, full of gentle perception and understanding, full of beauty and grace, full of joy unalterable."[25] A radical, she lived in "loving disagreement" with both church and government. Eileen Egan notes, "Gospel nonviolence rested on her belief in the unity of the human family."[26]

Etty Hillesum (1914–1943)

Esther (Etty) Hillesum was born January 15, 1914, in the Netherlands to a Dutch father and a Russian mother. Hillesum's father had his doctorate in classical languages, so she grew up surrounded by literature and the classics. She first did a law degree and then studied Slavonic languages, including Russian. In 1943, at age 29, she was killed in the gas chambers in a German concentration camp.

From 1941 to 1943, when it was a foregone conclusion that, as a Jew, she would be killed by the Nazis, Hillesum began keeping a diary of her daily life: in particular, of her journey into forgiveness of her enemy, her eventual murderers. She wanted every word she wrote to be essential. She hid her diary and just before her death gave it to friends with the express desire that it be published. Although many efforts were made to do so, it was not published until 1983, under the title *Etty: A Diary, 1941–43*. She wrote about "the slow and painful process of striving after inner freedom,"[27] noting that "mysticism must rest on crystal clear honesty and can only come after things have been stripped down to their naked reality."[28]

Over her two years of journalling, Hillesum reflected on what was burgeoning inside her: "a gradual change from the physical to the spiritual, and my own philosophy now, one I'm prepared to speak up for."[29] She spoke of both her desire to write and her writing as "spinning my thread…like a continuous line … a place from which one continues to spin one and the same thread, where one can gradually create a continuum which is really one's life."[30] Hillesum wanted to leave a record of her journey into peace and forgiveness. "O God, take me into your great hands and turn me into your instrument; let me write."[31] Her diary ended just before her death in Auschwitz on November 30, 1943.

The initial journal entries note her hatred of the Germans for what they were doing, and her conviction that there had to be another way to look at what was happening. Her March 21, 1941, entry shows her coming to grips with her life and the importance of living today as the only "real thing" there is. "I live here-and-now, this minute, this day, to the full and life is worth living."[32]

One of her frequent sayings was "Life is beautiful." A very sensuous woman, she saw the beauty of life in her sexuality; her diary is full of her erotic pleasures and love affairs. At one point, she realized that she also had to nurture her spirit. She began a life of prayer, with an hour of meditation daily.

Her journey into inner freedom had its own ebb and flow, as noted in her November 10, 1941, entry, wherein she expresses her panic, her lack of self-confidence and her aversion to what was happening.[33] Then, in her November 21 entry, she says, "Something is happening to me…. God take me by your hand. I shall follow dutifully and not resist too much."[34]

In 1942, Hillesum wanted to be with the Jews being transported to Westerbork concentration camp, believing she could live life totally in the present if she did not abandon her people in danger. She used her strength to bring joy to those living in fear and threat of the weekly transport train leaving for Auschwitz. Recognizing that life would be hard and that they would be separated, Hillesum could still say in her February 27, 1942, entry, "If you have a rich inner life… there probably isn't all that much difference between the inside and the outside of the camp."[35] Later she wrote in her diary, "I feel so sure of myself and not in the least afraid."[36]

Living each hour as though it were her last transformed Hillesum's hatred of the Germans to sorrow, a universal feeling for both the Jews and the Germans. In 1942, a year after she had begun her diary, she was able to say, "Do not relieve your feelings through hatred, do not seek to be avenged on all German mothers for they, too, sorrow at this very moment for their slain and murdered sons."[37] Living with such sorrow gives it that sacred space essential for healing. Otherwise, hatred and revenge violate that inner space, wreaking more sorrow, hatred and revenge. "If you have given sorrow the space its gentle origins demand, then you may truly say, life is beautiful and rich."[38]

Hillesum distinguished later in her diary between hatred and indignation, noting that hatred can be petty, with passing incidents being excuses for hatred. Indignation, on the other hand, must run deep and get to the core issues of injustice, violence and oppression.[39] Hillesum's inner freedom and lack of fear continued as the Jewish atrocities increased. Although she still spoke about her fear of when her time would come, and her inability to pray at this time, she continued to write and to hope, noting that "true peace will come when every individual finds peace within."[40]

As more people were loaded onto the transport trucks to Poland and to death, Hillesum was able to say yet again, "I know what may lie in wait for us.... And yet I find life beautiful and meaningful."[41] By July 1942, she was preparing herself for her own death for she had come to the realization that the Germans were going to annihilate them all. She spoke about becoming calmer and calmer in the face of death, realizing "the reality of death has become a definite part of my life."[42]

Knowing of the horrors of the gas chambers, Hillesum stated, "I keep finding myself in prayer. And that is something I shall always be able to do, even in the smallest space: pray."[43] Now, her entries became more prayers of praise and thanksgiving to God. She could say to God, "I know God, how much you have given me, so much that was beautiful and so much that was hard to bear. Yet, whenever I showed myself ready to bear it, the hard was transformed into the beautiful."[44]

In the end, Hillesum lived a very short life, yet she modelled love of enemy in ways that seem unreal today. Her journal entries show her constant movement into a way of life, a spirituality of nonviolence, that was both spiritual and concrete. Her journey from hatred to a deep inner freedom and peace matured as her prayer life matured. She lived in the present, and found life beautiful, seeing writing about her life as instructive for future generations.

Leonard Desroches 1948–

Leonard Desroches was born in 1948 in Penetanguishene, Ontario. A Franco-Ontarian, he speaks both French and English fluently. His book *Allow the Water* (1996) is a comprehensive text on the spirituality and practice of nonviolence, as well as an unofficial autobiography, particularly of his early and most formative years. Desroches describes himself as a very shy child who loved nature. He had a vivid imagination, creating a fantasy world where he could be at ease in the sheer essence of nature. With this deep love of creation, he sensed at a tender age the interconnectedness of all life species.

> I'd felt the powerful, mysterious presence of God in the community of sky, water, soil, plants and animals. I was beginning to feel the equally powerful, equally mysterious presence of God in the human community. 'La baie' (Georgian Bay) and 'love your enemies' seemed to embrace forever. I too, was indelibly embraced.... I sensed back then, in a childlike but essential way, that this kind of radical love was necessary for my spiritual survival. [45]

At his Catholic elementary school, he recalls being shaken when he learned through the Beatitudes about love of one's enemies. This epiphany at a young age was challenged in high school, where he was teased about speaking French. His indignation and rage boiled over one day in the washroom: he pushed the head of one of the worst teasers into the urinal and flushed it. He realized then the lure of what he came to call the power of violence. He also reflected, "It all seemed so utterly useless."[46]

Later, in a major seminary in the United States, Desroches saw Martin Luther King speaking on television about nonviolence in the face of the oppressive violence that was so much a part of the civil rights movement.

Something happened to me. I experienced…for the first time in my entire life what the capacity to face hatred without hating is really all about. I had finally begun a very long journey of discovering the other power, the power of nonviolence – power with, not power over. My spiritual longing and aching for what I now call simply the "other power" was finally being addressed … a very much unknown and untaught history.[47]

He left the seminary to continue what has become his life work: living and teaching the spirituality of nonviolence. Though he works as a drywaller by trade, he also spends a great deal of time working with individuals and groups, and writing about the spirituality of nonviolence in dealing with conflict.

At one point, while trying to explain to his aging mother what he did, Desroches shared his life commitment to nonviolence:

There were the obvious external dimensions – the resistance, the fasts, the arrests, the financial insecurity, the retreats, the writing and the workshops. But I realized that I'd never directly expressed what was the heart of it all for me…essentially, it's an attempt to learn what it actually means to love my enemies.[48]

Desroches is clear on the concrete aspects of the spirituality of nonviolence. He often says, "My enemy is one who is different enough from me to threaten me, make me afraid and angry. My enemy reflects back to me all of my own unresolved pain, fear and anger issues. My enemy is the one who confronts me with daily life choices. My enemy touches part of my broken self."[49]

Nonviolence involves becoming free in the core of one's being, even in the midst of pain, fear and anger, to the point where these are transformed into a force for nonviolent transformation. Freedom is being able to use anger as a catalyst for change, turning it into a force to resist evil, heal the wounded and nurture all life. In the end, such freedom frees us from dependency on violence and power over others.

Desroches' consciousness-raising within himself and with others has been a constant in his life, particularly regarding both the government's and church's belief in the Just War theory. At the time of the first Gulf War, and Canada's involvement in it, he engaged in a three-week fast in a public prayer space. He invited others to join him in his opposition to the war and its devastating effects on innocent people. He challenged Canada to stop running away from the truth: "We are a war-making country, ready to commit mass murder for the USA's oil."[50]

His second book, *Love of Enemy: The Cross and Sword Trial,* is a deeply moving account of his nonviolent resistance to a statue symbolizing the church's Just War teaching. In 1998, en route to strategize with others about resistance to Canada's possible involvement in a second bombing of Iraq, he passed by the cross and sword statue on the grounds of St. Paul's Anglican Church in Toronto. It became clear to him that the cross had been co-opted by the sword to justify the most organized form of violence: war. Although aware of his strong feelings related to the sword, he notes, "I truly was surprised by the sheer torrent in my soul. I stopped everything that I was doing and spent many hours in prayer and discernment."[51] Out of this discernment came the realization that after many years of carefronting war-making by corporations and governments, he had to carefront his own church community's sanctification of war by the false doctrine of the Just War theory. (See more about "carefrontation" in Chapter 6.)

Desroches considered the sword a blasphemy and a contradiction of what Jesus did on the cross, since the sword suggested victory by violence and war. The sword superimposed on the cross was "the clearest symbol of the Just War teachings of the mainline churches."[52]

He invited his church community to join him in an act of nonviolent resistance to the mainline churches' complicity in war. Two friends, Bob Holmes, a Roman Catholic priest, and Don Heap, an Anglican priest, joined Desroches in an attempt to remove the sword from the statue. The trio were arrested and charged with a criminal offence that carries a possible sentence of six months to ten years. A major trial followed a year later.

Desroches and his two colleagues exemplified the essence of the spirituality of nonviolence, eliminating any notion that this was a mere tactic. They developed strategies for nonviolent civil disobedience only after they had eliminated all the legal means possible to have the sword removed from the cross by the church. Desroches was able to say in the midst of his prayer, fasts, demonstrations and arrests, as well as the stress and agony of the trial itself, "Freedom from fear is freedom from violence."[53]

The trial, which lasted from 1998 to 2000, brought international attention to the church's complicity in perpetuating the Just War teaching. (Desroches and his friends were found guilty but given an unconditional discharge.) The trial also drew a whole array of supporters, lay and religious (including US Catholic bishop Thomas Gumbleton), and peacemaking groups from the US, Central America and Canada. The spirituality of nonviolence received media coverage. Desroches, with his friends, brought his own words to life: "No book, no retreat can convert us to nonviolence. We have to open a deep space for grace to move in our lives. We have to allow Christ to fully confront our deepest fears and our deepest yearnings."[54]

Desroches has moved from the intrapersonal to the interpersonal to the international in his spirituality of nonviolence. Over and over again, he expresses his opposition to what he calls the false doctrine of the Just War, which is endorsed by both church and state as the means to freedom. He notes that in the Sermon on the Mount (Matthew 5:43-48), right after calling us to love our enemies, Jesus calls us to be as mature in our love as God is.

To become mature, rather than perfect, is a process of becoming freer to renounce violence and the fear and greed that drive it. Desroches suggests that our clinging, officially and unofficially, to the Just War theory undermines all our works of charity, justice and mercy. We remain childish or adolescent in our collective love, in the face of the daily brutality and impoverishment war inflicts. His is a searing challenge to the church and us: "I personally do not know anyone who is deeply challenged or inspired by the pronouncements of such a compromised church which has barely begun to live out the radical, life-giving love of enemy."[55]

Desroches explores power at length, both in his writing and in his talks and training sessions. For many people, sharing power is undesirable. In hierarchical organizations, power is a scarce commodity, with barely enough for the ones who have made their way to the top of the pyramid. From this perspective, power is "power over." As Desroches notes, "There is possibly no more misused or abused word than 'power.' So often it is used to denote something negative."[56]

In our new story of a cosmic home, our challenge is to realize that power increases when it is shared and becomes "power with." Such power implies a vulnerability and interdependence characteristic of a quantum universe. "As power with begins to point to community, community points to mutuality … sharing power in such a way that each participant in the relationship is called forth more fully to becoming…a whole person with integrity."[57]

Two Greek words are used to distinguish between these two expressions of power. *Exousia* is externally sanctioned, hierarchical "power over"; *dunamis* is inner "power with," the result of deep inner strength that transforms fear into agapic love. "Understanding nonviolent power is being awake to the difference between *dunamis* and *exousia*," Desroches says.[58] He adds that *dunamis* is "the inner God-given power that we are all created with – dignity; and *exousia* [is] socially sanctioned power, public authority which may or may not be good, depending on the extent to which is it used as radical service."[59]

Desroches is a perfect example of a modern-day prophet of nonviolence. He has used his prophetic call-response, this gift and this grace, in conjunction with his talents of speaking and writing about nonviolence, to touch many people. In his ongoing deepening of his spirituality of nonviolence, he sees nonviolence as the real strength in Jesus' Third Way.

Desroches continues to make these delicate connections of love of the Earth and love of one's enemy in his life through prayer, utter simplicity, tolerance and joy. As a true prophet of nonviolence, he also fasts and demonstrates; like other prophets, he has been jailed, humiliated and put on trial. To all this, he has responded with love for his enemy. And like other prophets before him, his Manifesto of Nonviolence reiterates his spirituality of nonviolence.

> I am totally and unreservedly opposed to all expressions of violence, manipulation, lying deceit, and greed in myself, in others, in struc-tures. I commit my whole being to compassionately understanding the causes and sources of especially unconscious forms of violence, ma-nipulation,… but also resisting, denouncing, exposing, boycotting this violence, manipulation, lying deceit, and greed…. My motivations are love of myself, of every sister and brother, and a burning hunger to help reveal God as expressed in Jesus' liberating truth, life-giving justice and indestructible love.[60]

Reflection

The parable of the sower and the seed (Matthew 13:3-8) may help you reflect on the spirituality of nonviolence. When Jesus taught, he often spoke in parables so that, through the poetry of the prophetic imagination, the relevance of his message would be readily available.

The sower is God (the higher power in one's life), sowing the seed of God's es-sence. In the case of the four prophets we just met, that seed is the agapic love of God as expressed in the Sermon on the Mount: love your enemy. They all were deeply touched by this challenging and searing message.

However one truly learns to love one's enemy – with mature love that loves ac-tively but nonviolently – the seed of nonviolence is the same. The parable of the sower and the seed is a metaphor for the Sower God testing and working the soil of the lives of these prophets from scattered roadsides, rocky places, thorns and eventually the lush rich soil of their hearts. As we continue our own journey into a spirituality of nonviolence, and allow these prophetic sowers of nonviolence to seed the soil of our own hearts, we too become transformed into sowers.

In the end, each of us must nurture the spirituality of nonviolence in our lives with the good soil that will foster its growth. As Bishop Thomas Gumbleton, one of the witnesses at Leonard Desroches' cross and sword trial, said in another context, "We can't become nonviolent on the basis of intellectual conviction. Commitment to nonviolence demands a very profound conversion of mind and heart. If we take the time to pray with Jesus, we too will be converted in mind and heart. The only way is through a change of heart, a coming into a way of being that is the way of Jesus."[61]

Jesus' Third Way

In the Christian tradition, Jesus is the ultimate prophet of the spirituality of nonviolence.

Through the early stages of our evolution, when we did not have the capability of communicating well during conflicts, we had two instincts: fight when we thought we could win, or flight when we sensed we would lose.

Jesus' alternative is an assertive, constructive response that respects the other person in a conflict and, at the same time, takes care of oneself. Leonard Desroches notes, "There are three general responses ... passivity, violent opposition and the third way of militant nonviolence articulated by Jesus. Jesus abhors both passivity and violence as responses. His is a third alternative not even touched by those options."[62] It is love of one's enemy. Jesus did not shy away from differences, from conflict; he showed us how to deal with these nonviolently. As Joseph Phelps puts it, "Jesus' form of fighting...involved nonviolence, a love of enemy in the midst of conflict, and a desire to bring about true peace."[63]

After the "Blessed are the…" section of the Sermon on the Mount, Jesus continues with his, "But I say to you" (5:22ff) admonitions. His words are unequivocal: "But

I say to you, love your enemies and pray for those who persecute you" (5:44). How can we do this?

Biblical exegetes have written volumes on Jesus' admonition not to resist evil. Some suggest that a certain passivity is found there.[64] However, Walter Wink suggests that Jesus' Third Way is the essence of this passage: "Do not react violently against the one who is evil…. Find a new third way that is neither cowardly submission nor violent reprisal."[65] Jesus' own life exemplified this Third Way in explicit detail, culminating in his trial, passion and death, when he prayed for his enemies: "Father, forgive them…" (Luke 23:34).

Jesus' Third Way is a nonviolent way of transforming differences, injustices and oppression. Our new story is about all of us together creating the whole: each part in the whole and the whole in each part. The spirit of nonviolence, as lived by Jesus and other prophets of nonviolence, is within each of us. Such a transformation can be ours as we integrate their spirit into our daily lives, aware of "the transformed person as the agent of a transformed society…(and) the practice of Christianity since its founding."[66]

PART II: REFLECTION AND DISCUSSION STARTERS

1. What is your definition of violence? Does it include harm to all life, including the Earth? Why or why not?

2. Do you agree that it is important to contextualize conflict and anger transformation within the spirituality of nonviolence and our new story of a cosmic quantum universe? Why or why not?

3. Do you think violence is learned or innate? Explain. What do you think of the mixed messages we receive about violence?

4. The spirituality of nonviolence is both a way of life and a practice. Discuss.

5. What has touched you about one or other of the four prophets chosen as role models of nonviolence? How do they exemplify the characteristics of a prophet? Do you know other prophets who speak to you and your life?

6. What do you think about Jesus' Third Way as the alternative to the fight or flight response still so common today?

PART III

CONFLICT

4

INTRAPERSONAL AND INTERPERSONAL CONFLICT

When difference becomes an issue,
conflict results.

Stephen W. Littlejohn

I thought everybody handled conflict the way I did: by talking things out. Imagine my shock when I found out that this is not the case! I had an altercation with a peer, who later asked me a favour. I said yes, but added that we needed to discuss what had just happened.

Complacently, she informed me there was nothing to talk about. In her family, they never talked about conflict afterwards but continued on with their lives as if nothing had ever happened. They showed their "kiss and make up" by word and deed. The conflict was over, period! Doing my laundry at the time, I was so amazed, I froze, my hand in midair, pouring the soap into the washer. To this day, I go back to that learning situation when I reflect on how each of us views and handles conflict.

Many books and articles on conflict underscore quick and easy tricks and win-lose parameters, yet deep down we know there are no quick fixes. The goal of

Part III is to point out that conflict is not about win-lose or win-win (currently called both-gain) scenarios. Rather, I suggest that conflict is about learning how to love our enemy.

What Is Conflict?

A world of consumerism promotes instant gratification, with media advertising hypnotizing us into a false sense that we do not need to work at our relationships. Someone, somewhere, has an easy solution for us. Because most of us are uncomfortable with conflict, the quicker and easier the fix, the better. The bad news is there are no quick fixes; the good news is that conflict is normal, natural and necessary.

Our interpersonal conflicts suggest many viewpoints on what constitutes conflict, as does the plethora of research on the subject. The causes and conditions suggested in the literature for both conflict and peace affect how conflict is defined, how the parties involved handle it, and its stages and functions. As two scholars write, "Obviously 'conflict' is for the most part a rubber concept, being stretched and molded for the purposes at hand. In its broadest sense, it seems to cover everything from war to choices between ice-cream sodas or sundaes."[1]

Is conflict positive or negative? The word *conflict* comes from the Latin *confligare*, to strike together. In conflict, then, we find both heat and light, or energy. What we do with such energy makes the difference; the purpose of this book is to teach nonviolent ways of using it. "Conflict as such is neither good nor bad," Jacob Bercovitch explains. "When dealt with appropriately, it may lead to progress and creation; when dealt with inappropriately, it may lead to violence and destruction."[2]

Interpersonal conflict occurs between two individuals whose goals are incompatible.[3] While most people believe that conflict can and must be avoided, the truth is that "conflict is inevitable, the source of growth, and an absolute necessity if one is to be alive."[4]

Although conflict may feel threatening, the challenge is learning to deal with our differences as they arise, thus forestalling the destructive aspects of conflict.

Intrapersonal Conflict

> *Most conflicts with others extend from conflicts within ourselves.*
>
> Richard J. Mayer

I believe that most conflict begins intrapersonally – within, not outside, ourselves. It is not my intention here to link intrapersonal conflict with any deep-seated personality or psychological problems. On the contrary, this type of conflict is a normal aspect of our ongoing maturation. An integral part of the human condition, conflict's roots are in those physical, psychological and spiritual areas of ourselves where there are sparks of "unfinishedness" calling for more integration. These tug at us, clamouring for balance, self-love, self-esteem, self-acceptance, tolerance and openness. When we are unable to find some measure of balance and peace, we find ourselves in intrapersonal conflict.

When we define this type of conflict as a normal, natural and necessary part of each of us, we see it as part of our journey to wholeness and holiness. Intrapersonal conflict is all about recognizing the incompleteness of the human condition and ourselves as part of it. Transforming this type of conflict involves learning to deal with this incompleteness with love, acceptance and equanimity. When we do so, we will become able to grant that same space of openness and tolerance to our neighbour in our interpersonal conflicts. Wendy Grant asserts, "Before we can hope to resolve conflict with others, we first have to deal with our inner conflict that does, and will affect our behaviour and thought processes."[5]

Intrapersonal conflict must be an integral part of any discussion of conflict because, as Gini Graham Scott says, "Fears and inner conflicts prevent you from expressing what you really want to say or what you mean in a[n interpersonal] conflict situation."[6]

Where do you start? Many conflict definitions begin with interpersonal conflict, but I think we must start by looking within, because if we do not deal effectively with our inner conflict, it will aggravate interpersonal conflicts.

Interpersonal Conflict

> *Denying a conflict's existence*
> *does not cause it to go away;*
> *forced underground,*
> *it will eat away at our foundations.*
>
> David Cormack

Interpersonal conflict – between two or more parties who believe they have incompatible goals – is the most commonly recognized type of conflict. By the time we are more socially adept, we already have had several years of teaching on conflict, primarily through osmosis from parents, siblings, religion, teachers and society. I further define interpersonal conflict as differences that have become an issue between two people, related to resources, needs and values. Differences are not the cause of the conflict; they are part of the web of life's beauty, creativity and mystery. Rather, a conflict occurs when the differences between us have become problematic.

Each conflict has energy and spark. What we do with that energy determines whether it is more positive or negative: most conflicts have an ebb and flow of both qualities.

Interpersonal conflicts may happen between two people or small groups, or they may extend to larger entities, such as civil and international wars.

What issues lead to our interpersonal conflicts? In *relationship conflicts* with family, friends or colleagues, discontent is accompanied by strong emotions, misperceptions and poor communication. *Interest conflicts* involve competition over scarce resources, such as can be seen in companies and organizations. *Structural conflicts* reveal destructive behaviour patterns around goals and functions related to inequalities in power, control and ownership in pyramidal organizations. *Value conflicts* include incompatible beliefs about reality: different ways of being and doing, different criteria for evaluating behaviours or ideas.

The challenge of interpersonal conflicts is learning how to transform their energies of difference into some kind of balance. With experience, we can learn to live into our fears around our conflicts (accepting our intrapersonal conflicts has a tremendous bearing on this) and move with their energy. This energy becomes the catalyst for our transformation.

Interpersonal conflict can take different forms: constructive or productive; destructive; indirect; realistic or nonrealistic; disruptive or nondisruptive; subjective or objective.

Constructive or productive conflict is approached from a more positive stance. With greater flexibility in our behaviour, we are open to several ways of dealing with the conflict, thus transforming our differences. Folger and Poole point out, "Although parties…hold to their positions strongly, they are also open to movement if they become convinced that such movement will result in the best decision."[7]

Destructive conflict is based on our "old story," the worldview most of us were trained in, and our more familiar lens. We may try to avoid the conflict; when we cannot avoid it, we may insist we are right. This results in a more negative stance toward the other person. We are closed to new possibilities that could focus both our needs. The conflict becomes a "power over" situation, in which each of us holds on to our positions rather than our mutual needs. We become entrenched in our positions. "Conflicts are destructive if the participants are dissatisfied with the outcomes and think they have lost," explain Hocker and Wilmot.[8]

Indirect conflict results when people find it difficult to deal with conflict overtly. Because of ingrained norms and taboos about direct confrontation (impoliteness, immaturity, irrationality, sinfulness), indirect means may be used to deny conflict, including flight from the situation with passive or passive-aggressive behaviours or both. Ironically, "indirect conflicts have the longest life expectancy, and have the most costs that cannot be charged back against the original conflict."[9]

A *realistic conflict* occurs when one person interferes with another's attainment of a specific goal. In contrast, a *nonrealistic conflict* has little or nothing to do with the situation at hand, and a lot to do with our unresolved tension and frustration from other situations: "the straw that breaks the camel's back."

Disruptive conflict, an exchange of opposing perspectives, interferes with group energy. *Nondisruptive conflict*, which does not interrupt the normal flow of the group, is also called "pseudo-conflict."[10]

Some make a distinction between *subjective* and *objective conflict*. A subjective or narrow approach to conflict focuses on values, motivations and attitudes of the individuals concerned, whereas an objective or wider approach stresses the structural or systemic factors of a given conflict. Dealing with conflict from a subjective perspective focuses on the individuals' changing their perceptions of the parameters of the conflict. An objective perspective entails a fundamental restructuring of the whole system.

Deep-rooted conflict is complex and sacred, and has to do with a person, group or nation's identity. To recognize it in our own lives, we must understand it well. It is not readily managed or resolved, because it is linked to the essence of who we are.

Because of its vital connection to self-identity and interiority, its structures of violence are mimetic – they try to imitate an ideal. People's words ("I have to do this for my religion, my country, my family") and accompanying actions are coupled with fear, resentment and hatred. People are oriented toward death and destruction – even their own death if this will eliminate the enemy. Because the enemy has been demonized, such acts are seen as heroic, even saintly. It is the nature of these conflicts to be intractable, interminable, self-sustaining and self-perpetuating. They have a certain stability and can continue for generations.

Each of us can cite examples of deep-rooted conflict, perhaps in our own family. Sometimes we can no longer recall the origins of the conflict. It is a matter of honour to keep the conflict going. Pearce and Littlejohn explain, "The original cause becomes irrelevant and new causes for conflict are generated by the actions within the conflict itself,"[11] even with attempts at resolving the conflict, which become cause for continuing the conflict.

Ebb and Flow of Conflict

Four Principles of Conflict

A basic understanding of conflict is critical because such learning helps determine how you respond: after the fact and, eventually, during the conflict. Understanding helps us eliminate fear around conflict.

Interpersonal conflict, which is interactive by nature, reflects the energy of both parties in a cycle of initiation, response and counter-response. Once a conflict begins, it can take on various nuances: it can be suppressed, avoided, denied or constructively managed. From this ebb and flow, four principles of conflict have emerged:

1. Patterns of behaviour in conflict tend to perpetuate themselves.

2. As senseless and chaotic as a conflict interaction may appear, it has a general direction that can be understood.

3. Conflict interaction is sustained by the moves and countermoves of participants.

4. Conflict interaction affects the relationships between participants.[12]

The Stages of Conflict

Although we will look at conflict "stages," this term is a social construct. In fact, the conflict process is a very fluid rather than a linear reality.

Conflict is always present, just under the surface of any situation. Its *latency* stems from our distinct viewpoints, goals, needs and values. It takes a *triggering event* to spark differences to the point where they become problematic. For example, you and I may have differences around quality time spent with each other. These latent differences become activated by the triggering event in which you decide that the football game on TV is more important than our watching a movie together. This triggering event, in which I feel like I am second fiddle, activates certain behaviours in both of us. I may sulk and give you the silent treatment; you may turn off the TV and leave. Immediately or later, these actions become the issues and triggering events for the next cycle. Because of the ebb and flow of the energy in conflict, the *acknowledged conflict stage* has its own energy and time and is followed by a *de-escalation* phase, accompanied by a transformation of this energy, such as resolving the conflict or simply managing it. At all times, there is the desire that some kind of mutual growth will occur in the transformation of its energy.

Cycle after cycle of conflict occurs when substantive and affective differences become issues.

The metaphor of conflict as a three-act play, usually with an encore, is another way of picturing conflict, according to Jeffrey Rubin.[13] *Act One*: Beginning and Escalation; *Act Two*: Climax and Stalemate; *Act Three*: De-escalation and Termination. In other words, conflict chaos has a certain order and predictability in its disorder. It does have boundaries.

In Act One, the conflict escalates when differing needs, values and resources become problematic, and continues with the two parties turning their initial criticism of each other into attacks on each other's personalities. In Act One, things tend to heat up.

In Act Two, the conflict reaches a climax, the point where the principals run out of steam and insults. It is a reprieve, a stalemate, but that does not mean that either side is any less determined to win.

With Act Three, there is a movement to termination, a de-escalation and some kind of settlement – at least for now, since all conflict is latent. The triggering event for the next play is just around the corner.

In another model of the conflict process, Louis Kriesberg describes the four stages of conflict as awareness, escalation, de-escalation and termination.[14] The fluidity of these stages depends on several factors, including the parties' awareness of incompatibility, the intensity of their feelings and behaviours, the extent to which the conflict is regulated or institutionalized, the balance of power between the parties, and the "purity" of the conflict.

The spiral effect is another model of conflict.[15] This model highlights the different aspects of conflict and emphasizes its ongoing nature, beginning with pressure and threat, then spiralling to overt conflict, relationship changes, further escalation of differences leading to more conflict. The spiral continues until the parties involved can sidestep it and move to another way of interacting.

At this point, you are probably sifting through the conflicts in your own life, recognizing there are various levels and intensities of conflict. Speed Leas outlines five levels of conflict,[16] with specific attention given to the issues and emotions at each level. Level 1 is the easiest conflict; Level 5 is an intractable conflict. There is no one way to deal with conflict because there are different types of, and different energies in, conflict, all based on varying needs, resources and values, to say nothing of culture, gender and power issues. As you read through the list, see whether you can remember a conflict in your own life that might fit each level.

Level 1: Problems to Solve. The objective is to work out a solution to the problem. There is no hidden agenda; the focus is the here and now. Communication is open and the principals want an amicable solution to their differences. This type of conflict is the easiest to transform.

Level 2: Disagreements. The objective becomes nuanced with a need for self-protection. Here there is a mixing of the issues with the personalities involved. The communication moves to making generalizations ("You always, never…").

There are overtones of distrust beginning but this type of conflict can still be transformed with relative ease.

Level 3: Contests. The objective is winning and putting the "enemy" in her or his place. There are personal attacks in this win/lose situation. The communication becomes more closed with no sharing of emotions. This type of conflict is tough to transform.

Level 4: Fight/Flight. The objective is hurting one's enemy in some way, getting rid of the person. The shift is from winning to getting rid of the enemy. The communication is self-righteous and "right" versus "wrong." This level of conflict is very difficult to transform.

Level 5: Intractable Situations. The objective is to destroy one's enemy, irrespective of the cost to self or the enemy. The conflict here is unmanageable, protracted and the other is seen as harmful. Communication is very vindictive, self-righteous. This level of conflict is seen by most as impossible to transform. As detailed earlier, deep-rooted, moral conflicts are of this type, requiring new organic and systemic ways of approaching them.

The following table summarizes our discussion about the cycle of conflict, integrating the stages of conflict from three theorists with similar views.

TABLE — CONFLICT STAGES

FOLGER & POOLE	KRIESBURG	CORMACK
1. latent conflict		1. threat, pressure
2. conscious of opposition	1. awareness of conflict	2. separation
3. triggering event(s)	2. escalation	3. divergence
4. acknowledged conflict		4. conflict
		5. disorganisation
		6. disintegration
		7. escalation
	3. de-escalation	
	4. termination	
		8. more threat, pressure, etc

Definitions of conflict sit on a continuum, ranging from positive to negative. Balance is the middle of the road. When viewed negatively, conflict is always destructive, a zero-sum game in which there are winners and losers. A scarcity of resources, wealth, status, power and esteem, as well as different needs and values, results in competition, coercion, force and violence. The final outcome is "power over" and oppression. When viewed positively, conflict becomes a transformative situation worked out through cooperation and mutuality, with respect for differences. The reality of conflict, for most of us, is probably somewhere between these two extremes, with both positive and negative potential.

From the above discussion, we may have the sense that conflict occurs in distinct linear stages. But from a quantum perspective, conflict is really about energy, which has nothing to do with levels and stages. However, such an overview does help us see patterns. The emotional, intuitive right brain knows the ineffable flow of the energy of conflict, both from our own experience and from our observation of others. At the same time, the analytical left brain may need a logical, linear view of conflict to name an elusive reality. Noting the interconnections between our intrapersonal and interpersonal conflicts in a quantum universe, it is perhaps more precise to say that "conflicts are more like a seamless web with indistinguishable beginnings and endings."[17]

5

THE COMPLEXITY OF CONFLICT

Conflict is complex, with many variables – including culture, stress, personality, self-esteem, gender, power and group development – affecting its outcome. I focus on each briefly here, with references for personal follow-up.

Conflict and Culture

> *Cultural divergence becomes painful in conflict*
> *situations when others challenge our common*
> *expectations about how to proceed.*
>
> Barnett Pearce

What Is Culture?

Culture, from the Latin *cultus* and *cultare,* has a number of meanings, including worshipping, tilling and cultivating. At one time, culture was considered to be the fixed, static essence of a particular group. The people in the group belonged to this particular culture and no other, and they all defined and experienced their culture in the same way (ethnocentrism).

How does culture affect the way you see conflict? Conflict does not occur in a vacuum; it is framed within the learned pattern of norms and taboos related to our thoughts, values and behaviours. Culture itself can be a main source of conflict, as is seen vividly in the conflicts in Northern Ireland, the Middle East, Africa, Afghanistan and Iraq.

Culture can be defined along a continuum from shared values, to the way things are done, to a system of values, laws, ideologies and day-to-day rituals, to an organization which has a number of 'cultural' elements, including values, rituals and communication networks. According to Terence Deal, "Culture is a concept that captures the subtle, intangible, largely unconscious forces that shape a society or a workplace ... social fiction created by people to give meaning to work and life."[1] In other words, culture is the set of values and assumptions that suggest norms and taboos for the way things are done. Such usages of culture stem from a nineteenth century notion of culture, seen as a whole, integrated, universal system, specific to race, language and worldview.

Culture: Social Construction

Today in our cosmic community, we are learning to see culture much more broadly, with three interacting primary components: a material culture directly dependent on our ecosystem; a social culture of kith and kin, politics and economics; and a sacred culture of beliefs, myths and rituals that give meaning to our lives.[2]

Much of the North American literature on conflict homogenizes all aspects of conflict, despite the several cultures to which each of us belongs and the different experiences people have of the same culture. Each person experiences her or his culture differently from every other person of that culture, due in part to that person's belonging to other cultures, as well as her or his personality, intrapersonal and interpersonal conflicts, and life experiences. For this reason, dealing with interpersonal conflict means ensuring that the individuals involved have the same understanding of the conflict, and, as Eggleton and Trafford point out, being "aware that cultural differences affect the way people communicate, the values they tend to take for granted, and their perceptions of any process of reconciliation and healing."[3]

Moving from the stability and stasis of our mechanistic worldview to the fluidity and change of an organic model affects our understanding of culture. Our worldview and our cultures must reflect the complexity of our new story. Culture is not timeless, nor solely about customs and traditions. Rather, it is a set of complex and complicated cognitive, perceptual, emotional and spiritual processes.

Enculturation, Acculturation and Inculturation

We speak of *enculturation* as the process of absorbing the ways of being and doing in our primary culture, an osmosis that is largely unconscious. *Acculturation* is our going to another culture, with its ways of being and doing. It is putting aside the familiar and, at the same time, comparing and contrasting the new culture's norms and taboos with those of our own primary culture. Having lived in various parts of Canada, the United States, Europe and Japan, I have found that we could improve certain ways of doing things in my primary culture and that I prefer certain Canadian ways to those of other cultures. As I became acculturated in new cultures, I became more enculturated in my own culture.

All cultures recognize a higher being. According to Benedictine Joan Chittister, "Seeking God is the universal human quest. It is common to all cultures. It is the fundamental human project. It is the common denominator of the human enterprises."[4] *Inculturation*, a theological term, is a recognition and acceptance of God, as God is named and worshipped in other cultures. It is an attempt to move away from the model where one imposes cultural norms about God, religion and spirituality on another culture.

Conflict and Stress

> *Fear creates stress...*
> *which can manifest itself as conflict.*
>
> Wendy Grant

What Is Stress?

Stress (from the Latin *stringere,* to pull, draw tight) is a constant in our lives. Stress is our response to change. In the Chinese culture, the word "crisis" is denoted by two characters: *wei-chi* ("danger" and "hidden opportunity for change"). In the West, when we experience a crisis and its attendant stress, we see the danger, but rarely recognize the opportunity. "If we resist change," says Kristine C. Brewer, "we create stress, more harmful to us than the change itself."[5]

Physiologically, when the brain interprets that we are in stress because of the pressure of a change (good or bad), the body goes into fight or flight mode. The brain initiates a whole physiological chain reaction within the body with the release of adrenaline and noradrenaline into the bloodstream, automatically determining the amount of each, according to the threat. This short-term response is designed to help us flee or fight the danger. The heart pounds, sugar increases, the blood clots, pupils are dilated, face pales or flushes, muscles tense and breathing becomes quick and shallow.

Our bodies are programmed for homeostasis (equilibrium). Anything perceived as a threat to the status quo is potentially dangerous and stressful, pulling tightly on our bodies, minds and spirits. Our particular reaction to change and difficult situations is based on our personality and our emotional and physical makeup, as well as past experiences and the stress of the present situation.

Types of Stress

But stress is not all bad; there is also good stress, called *eustress,* integral to any living organism. For Kristine Brewer, "Positive stress help us to concentrate, focus, and perform and often helps us reach peak and efficiency."[6] This is the stretching that challenges us to get out of bed in the morning and keeps us motivated to be, learn, do and grow. Without it, many of us would not have that inner drive.

Distress means to be stretched apart. Brewer explains, "Stress becomes negative when we stay geared up and won't – can't – relax after meeting the challenge."[7] Chronic or prolonged stress, manifested in a series of physiological processes called the General Adaptation Syndrome, is problematic. When we react too strongly to arousal, excitement, challenge or frustration, the body pumps more and more adrenaline, noradrenaline and cortisol into the bloodstream, keeping us in a high state of alert. We can function at this level only for a certain period of time before our system crashes, resulting in burnout, chronic fatigue, depression or other health problems. Today, we hear a great deal about stress in the workplace, with some studies claiming that 75 per cent of workers feel stress on the job.[8] Admitting to such stress is seen as a weakness, a character flaw. In fact, it is suggested that 50 to 80 per cent of all illnesses are stress related.

Eustress and distress are part of our lives. If we can maintain some kind of balance between these two energies, stress will not be an exaggerated triggering factor for conflict in our lives. But if someone is carrying too much distress, this overload can turn differences (which might be recognized and accepted on one occasion) into a triggering event for conflict.

It is critical that we know ourselves, our intrapersonal conflicts and our stressors in order to identify the factors that are affecting a given interpersonal conflict situation. If we do not have this awareness, the urge to have control over something and someone can turn to violence in our interpersonal conflicts.

Conflict and Self-Esteem

> *Anxiety is a sign that one's*
> *self-esteem is endangered.*
>
> David Augsburger

What Is Self-Esteem?

Within our intrapersonal conflicts, and on our journey to integration and self-transcendence, we must know and love ourselves. Poor self-esteem can exacerbate hurts and slights, and make most of our differences an issue.

Self-esteem is our acceptance and love for ourselves, how we view ourselves despite what others may say. Nathaniel Branden, writing extensively on many aspects of self-esteem, reminds us, "Self-esteem…in the core of one's being…is a basic psychological need…a basic human need…essential to normal and healthy development."[9]

Each of us, with the input of significant others in our lives, has been shaping our self-image since childhood, even infancy. It is suggested that by the time we begin school, we have many "negative" tapes of ourselves, coming in large part from our home and family. Comments such as "You're not as pretty, smart, nice, generous…as your sister, brother" have been imprinted deep within our psyches. It is out of these experiences that we build our self-image.

Our self-image is the basis for our self-esteem. According to Wendy Grant, "a tremendous amount of inner conflict is caused by a sense of poor self-esteem."[10] The more love and care we have received for who we are, the more grounded is our self-esteem, and the more likely we are to resist negative labels that others try to give us.

My research and sessions on self-esteem indicate that it tends to be more of a concern for women than men.[11] In a subject-object dualistic worldview, many women have absorbed the notion of "object" rather than "subject."

Because women have bought into a certain external image of who they should be and what they should do, too many bright, successful and competent women are afraid of being labelled as pushy and aggressive, which leads to adverse consequences for their relationships.

The adage "Women have to be twice as good as men to go half as far" appears to be changing; some women are moving beyond such shackles, recognizing their gifts and talents in areas once seen as male bastions. (The converse is also happening.) Still, says Nathaniel Branden, "when self-esteem is weak, success can trigger anxiety…dread and disorientation…when career and work-life go well in ways that conflict with their deepest vision of who they are and what is appropriate to them."[12]

Some women are ambivalent toward their own success and professional advancement (The Impostor Syndrome). Some successful women believe, because of an underlying poor self-image and self-esteem, that they are fakes, who will imminently be found out. They have the sense that any success they achieve is purely by chance, by the luck of the draw. Only recently have some men been able to see the same phenomenon in themselves.[13]

In shame and fear, it is difficult not to believe someone with power, authority and status who tells us we have not measured up. For example, no matter what our age, when we hear a word or phrase that holds a great deal of emotional baggage, a voice or person from the past may surface in our hearts, confirming yet again what was said of old. We believe such messages, unless we have been able to put them to rest.

If we have worked on the essence of such feedback and have more fully integrated our self-identity and self-esteem by transforming such inner conflicts, we can assure ourselves from a grounded place within that the criticism is not true. However, according to Houel and Godefoy, "if our self-image is defective or fragile, we are much more vulnerable to attack."[14]

Being able to see the connection between our self-esteem and our intrapersonal and interpersonal conflicts is crucial. The more aware we are, the more we can deal with our intrapersonal conflicts in a healthy way, recognizing them as un-finished business and as latent energy for our interpersonal conflicts.

One of Jesus' teachings (Luke 10:25-28) exemplifies the importance of healthy self-esteem. A lawyer asked Jesus what to do to gain eternal life. Knowing a law-yer could probably quote the law, Jesus asked him what the law said about the matter. The man replied, "You shall love God with your whole heart, soul, mind, strength, and your neighbour as yourself." Jesus answered, "You have answered correctly. Now, go do it and you will live"!

I have heard many homilies on this Scripture passage. Most of them emphasized its first two aspects: love of God and love of neighbour. The third and, I think, the most important is the love of self, or self-esteem. We can love God and neighbour only to the extent that we love ourselves. Otherwise, such love could become narcissistic or egotistic, a love that has us performing acts of love out of self-adulation and underlying selfishness.

True love of self is difficult for many people, both women and men, given what our culture has taught us. Building self-esteem is the slow process of becoming and remaining a person made in God's image and likeness.

Conflict and Gender

> *In the dance of life, opposites create the ploy.*
> *Male is not better than female…*
> *Both are essential to the whole.*
>
> P. K. Metz, J. L. Tobin

Despite the changes effected by feminism in Western society, and despite the consciousness-raising around the social justice issue of sexism, women have been regarded as the second sex, misbegotten or deficient males.[15] Interestingly, the research has shown this "relative position of the sexes in each culture is always the same."[16] Today, some changes toward equality are happening.

Many women have been socialized to conform to sex-role stereotypes on numerous issues, including conflict. In a patriarchal and hierarchical system with its sex-role stereotyping and gender socialization, they are treated as objects.

Sex-role socialization and stereotyping begins early – even in utero. A number of cultures and religions place more value on male babies; girls are seen as inferior. The dualistic subtleties are noted in the clothes, games, toys, emotions, jobs and roles in society that are allotted to each sex. Tavris and Offir note, "Children are raised differently depending on their sex. Socialization takes place in many ways: through inadvertent as well as deliberate rewards and punishments and through language, media messages and adult examples."[17]

Although efforts to change all of this have begun in some instances, still we can say, along with Joan Chittister, a Catholic woman religious and feminist, "Patriarchy devalues women."[18] Humans are male or female, based on anatomical differences; gender is a social construct based on a patriarchal, hierarchical worldview, as summarized in the following table.

TABLE — DUALISTIC SEX-ROLE SOCIALIZATION

MALE	FEMALE
masculine	feminine
subject	object
rational	emotional
strong	weak
dominant	subordinate
right	wrong
independent	dependent
domineering	docile
separate	connected
helper	helpless
competitive	cooperative
winner	loser
superior	inferior

A subtle part of gender socialization concerns the handling of conflict. Many men, trained to be independent, competitive and separate, have been socialized to see conflict as a game, a battle to be won. It is viewed as a winner-take-all game with high stakes between dominants and subordinates, superiors and inferiors. For some men, handling conflict requires that the parties be rational, since any display of emotion is a sign of weakness and such a display will result in their losing their power.

In contrast, most women, socialized to be connected, relational, dependent, cooperative, and society's primary caregivers, are in a more vulnerable "object" position, particularly in conflicts with men. Women have very little power in the hierarchical institutions of which they are part (church, society, family, workplace) and, therefore, in how conflict is usually handled. (These dualistic terms are just that – social constructs that have become realities within our cultures. Most people tend to have a range of "masculine" and "feminine" qualities in varying degrees. Both women and men can find it frustrating when they feel forced to hide or defend qualities that have typically been linked to the other sex.)

One of the adverse side effects of such dualism is that women learn to handle conflicts, particularly with men, in more indirect ways, acting out of the specific norms and taboos of socialized gender differences. Women as objects have also learned to communicate their needs and wants indirectly because of fear of rejection, while men – as subjects and in control – are more direct. These differences can become the stuff of conflict. For example, a couple driving home from a meeting passes a café. She says, "Wouldn't you like to stop in for a coffee?" because she would like to do just that. He, taking her question literally, says, "No, I want to go right home." She is hurt because he was not sensitive to her needs, and yet she did not say what she wanted. Our ignorance and inability to move beyond our sex-role socialization can have adverse effects on relationships at every level.

When women feel they do not have any formal power in dualistic structures, they become very adept at seduction, manipulation and control, primarily through passive and passive-aggressive ways of communication. If, on the other hand, they are assertive in a situation in which these cultural norms and taboos are in effect, they become labelled by both men and women (women can collude with oppressive structures) because they dared to forget their place.

As we live our new story of equality, mutuality and interdependence, and experience the positive effects of such values on our relationships, including our interpersonal conflicts, the time has come for us to move away from dualism.

The time has come to speak about human qualities, recognizing both women and men have many of the qualities ascribed to the other sex.

Conflict and Power

> *Don't walk in front of me*
> *I may not follow.*
> *Don't walk behind me*
> *I may not lead.*
> *Walk beside me*
> *and just be my friend.*
>
> attributed to Albert Camus

Power Over, Power With

Is power a good thing in your life? How do you use your power? How has power been used on you? Have you ever experienced the seduction of power?

In any analysis of power, it is important to look at both its denotations and connotations. First, its denotations. Etymologically, power means possibility and potential. In many hierarchical systems, power is seen as a scarce commodity that diminishes when shared. In such pyramidal systems, with room for so few at the top, power's potential becomes "power over," characterized by manipulation and control by the "haves" over the "have nots." Such power over can become addictive: the more we try to control a person or system, the more it resists, which creates a cycle of violence.

Think about the many negative connotations of power: power-hungry, stealing power, powerless, disempowered, power-mongers. Yet we also refer to power in positive ways: as authority, strength, influence, psychic or charismatic force, vigour, physical force and energy. In our new story, in which we are all interdependent, power as possibility is life-giving. It is "power with," a nonviolent

THE COMPLEXITY OF CONFLICT ———————— 91

power, because it becomes a strength for the benefit of all. It entails both reverence of its potential and responsibility for its appropriate use.

"Power over" leads to competition, envy and obsession with success. Only when we can see power as "power with" can we avoid its seduction, corruption, violence, coercion, manipulation and oppression of others.

When two adults come together in a supposedly power-equal relationship, they assume that conflict can be handled overtly, constructively and nonviolently. However, each person brings a set of values to the relationship around such issues as power, division of labour, paid vs. unpaid work, and childcare. When their differences become an issue and conflict occurs, each person reacts and responds from learned behaviours. This means that one of the people in a couple may be seen as the inferior, and "power over" will be used to maintain the status quo. "Power over" and power imbalance go hand in hand, state Hocker and Wilmot, to the point that "parties continually struggle over their share of the pie – what the other gets, you lose."[19]

Domestic Violence

The United Nations Children's Fund estimates that up to half the women in the world suffer some kind of domestic violence at the hands of their husbands.[20] Domestic or family violence is a serious and prevalent type of intrafamily conflict that can take many forms, and has a clear link to "power over" by the male toward the female. "The primary victims of family violence are women, children, seniors and people with disabilities," reports *Origins*, a Catholic journal.[21] Most of the incidents we know about personally and from the media involve the abuse of women and children, because men are dominant in the structures in which the violence takes place. Rape and sexual assault are blatant examples of the perpetrator's desire and need for power. Stories of domestic violence are reported almost daily in our newspapers. One such article from London's *The Times* studying domestic violence noted that the major cause of men's violence towards their partners is power.[22]

Some chilling statistics were cited in this article. Of about 635,000 incidents of domestic violence a year, only one in five (1:5) is reported; these women have suffered some 30 attacks before they do anything about the assault. One in four (1:4) women suffer beatings, rape or ill-treatment at some point in their lives. Two women a week in England and Wales are murdered by a current or former husband or partner. Seventy (70) per cent of the incidents involve the abuser drinking. "The problem cuts across all racial and social backgrounds with many professional, successful and well-educated women suffering years of violence at the hands of men from similar backgrounds," the article adds.[23]

A distressing aspect of these grim statistics is that repeat offences are highest among perpetrators of domestic violence. "While therapeutic schemes for sex offenders, drug abusers, and violent criminals were generally seen as a success," says the article, "the offenders who seemed beyond treatment were those guilty of domestic violence."[24]

An important variable in domestic violence is the cycle of power over, oppression and abuse. Despite the plethora of sensitivity training sessions available for males, this same study noted that "a third of boys believed that some women deserved to be hit and half felt that women might have provoked the violence."[25]

Within dualistic structures, women may not know their rights or may even collude with such an oppressive system, as evidenced by a third of the women in the study who felt domestic violence might be acceptable in certain circumstances and half who felt that the violence did not in itself constitute sufficient reason for the relationship to end.[26] When women are seen both by their partners and themselves as inferior and needing to be kept in their place, they are coerced – physically, psychologically and spiritually – to be kept inferior when there is stress or tension in the relationship.

Rape is a clear example of "power over" behaviour. Inner stress and striving for power and control lead to the high incidence of rape and assault. During a discussion about power in a session I led on conflict and anger, a married man sadly realized that he raped his wife when he needed to feel power over or control in their marriage, such as when they had a conflict or when he felt powerless in other areas of his life, especially at work.

Rape is integral to the "power over" of war, along with plundering, assault and maiming. The sexual abuse by pedophiles, including clergy and other professionals whose mandate is a sacred trust to protect others, is another form of "power over."

"Power over" can take many forms, including damage done to a child's or partner's self-esteem and rights to safety, security and fulfillment. For conflict to be transformed, there must be a relative balance of power.

The last conflict variable we will explore is conflict as a stage in the life of a group.

Conflict and Group Development

A group cannot be cohesive
until it is able to deal with conflict.

Rosine Hammet and Loughlan Sofield

Many of us probably belong to several groups. A primary group, such as family, is connected by blood ties. A secondary group includes our professional and organizational affiliations. A third group, such as a community of consecrated women or men, is a group of adults gathered together to live out a spiritual mission.

Let us examine briefly the stages of group development, with particular attention given to the conflict stage, which is a critical turning point in the life of a group.

Forming

During the forming stage, we orient ourselves to others in the group. Here, our interpersonal and intragroup relationships are superficial, due to our desire to feel included and safe; we are polite, reticent and easygoing. In the words of Richard Weber, "The goal for the individual is to establish safe patterns for interaction."[27]

Storming

During the storming or conflict stage, there is sufficient safety and comfort for us to name the incompatibilities around such issues as control, power, leadership and goals. Because conflict is always latent, it takes a particular triggering event for the conflict to be brought out into the open. The conflict encourages us to look at our own behaviours and their effects on others in the group. We are used to looking at others' behaviours, not our own. Our lack of awareness of the fluid nature of any group may cause us to forget that we have a vital influence and effect on the group. Examining what we do or don't do in this conflict, and how we contributed to it in the first place, challenges us to take a closer look at our intrapersonal conflicts and our interpersonal relationships with others in the group.

This stage is the crux of any system's development. Here, many of the unnamed issues of our intrapersonal conflicts come to the fore and determine the nuances of the intragroup conflict. The conflict, in its inevitable progression, may escalate in different ways: with covert, passive, or passive-aggressive behaviours, or with direct behaviours, aggressive or assertive.

The conflict affects the whole group, and the group must handle it in some way. When group members try to escape from the unpleasantries of this stage, they will experience failure and return to this point again and again, until the process is completed, if ever. Conflict is the catalyst that moves the group through its stages, and may require facilitation or mediation from outside the group.

Part of moving forward as a group is being free enough, from deep within, to look at the ways of being and doing in the group. One of the major challenges is changing the group's unspoken norms and taboos. Change, tolerance and acceptance of differences are key attitudes. A group cannot fulfill its potential when the issues of the interpersonal and intragroup relationships are not explored in interdependent and mutual ways.

Norming

The dissatisfaction and conflict of the storming stage, with its escalation and eventual de-escalation, become the catalyst for the norming stage. Norming requires the group to look at the norms and taboos and change these to fit the interpersonal relationships among group members and how these, in turn, affect the intragroup identity. Here we must look at what needs to change for the group to be more cohesive. When this is not done, the conflict continues, at times underground. Without the change that norming involves, the group is stuck in a pattern of ongoing violence, oppression and abuse.

Performing/Transforming

Once a group has worked through its conflict stage and found healthy ways to relate, members move on to the performing stage. I prefer to call this the transforming stage. This wonderful, if transient, stage engenders trust, acceptance and nonviolence among group members, and can lead to members building deep relationships and even friendships. Due to its equilibrium and cohesiveness, the group moves forward with its goals and objectives rather than losing sight of them amid issues of power, control and violence.

This season of transforming differences releases energy that was previously tied up in negativity. The new ways of being and doing reflect the principles of our new story: equality, mutuality, reciprocity and respect. Grounded in these values, we are better prepared for the next conflict about to burst open in fluid and life-giving ways.

To Tuckman's four stages I have added two further stages: faith-forming and adjourning.

Faith-forming

"Faith-forming" is a separate stage, after transforming, particularly for religious groups. It is only at this stage of trust, tolerance and a sense of safety that we, as individuals, can share how God has been transforming us from the inside out. Since this sharing is about the core of our identity, it requires mutuality and reciprocity.

If the group has not done the hard work necessary to reach this level of trust, then this stage can be reduced to a subtle but insidious form of violence, where members resort to "power over" in order to shore up their crumbling spiritual life.

Adjourning

Adjourning marks the end of the life of any group. With a change of membership, it becomes a new group, and the process begins all over again.

Ritualizing our goodbyes is important, and adjourning is instrumental to the health of any group. I believe that when we cannot say goodbye, then we cannot say hello to the next experience. When we are not willing to face the pain and sorrow of loss, then we may not be open enough within our hearts to say hello to someone new who comes into our lives and into a group to which we belong.

The following table portrays a number ways of looking at the life of a group.

TABLE — STAGES OF GROUP DEVELOPMENT

TUCKMAN	SCHUTZ	LACOURSIERE
1. forming	1. inclusion	1. orientation
2. storming	2. control	2. dissatisfaction
3. norming	3. affection	3. resolution
4. performing (transforming)		4. production
(5. faith-forming)		
(6. adjourning)		5. termination

Conflict is a very real part of the life growth of any group. The advantage of the stages recurring again and again is that the group can consciously recognize them as they arise. In that way, the issues can be worked through more intentionally, more compassionately, more tolerantly and perhaps with less pain.

6

DEALING WITH CONFLICT

*It is the way that we respond to conflict which
determines whether the outcome of that conflict is
creative and healthy, or limiting and unhealthy.*

Martin Eggleton

What Is Your Style?

How do you handle conflict? Various factors – including your worldview, culture(s), sex, power, the complexity of the conflict issues, your affective state, and the people involved – determine your approach.

The *cognitive approach* focuses on the individuals and their relationship. Since conflict is about different needs, values and perceptions, this approach emphasizes the relationship between the two people and looks at how they can manage their differences in ways that can preserve the relationship. It highlights their working together, moving to the needs of each so that they decide together what the problem is, related to their differences; establish the outcome they want; and determine how they can best realize this outcome together.[1]

The *institutional approach* looks at conflict within an organization in a particular culture, suggesting change needed in the institution's ways of being and doing. Because of the inherent hierarchy, the numbers of people involved and the unwillingness of those at the top to share power, such change involves considerable time and re-education.

The *game theory approach* is perhaps the one with which we are most familiar. In a game, the two sides use a series of moves and counter-moves to win. In the soft-game approach, the players are more like friends: they are willing to negotiate the tension in their relationships and their needs or interests. In the hard-game approach, on the other hand, the players are enemies and the competition is fierce.

A significant number of theoreticians and practitioners use the game theory approach to conflict, with adaptations of Blake and Mouton's five-part typology and its two variables of cooperation and assertiveness:

*competition

*accommodation

*avoidance

*problem solving

*compromise.

Whetten et al. (1996) and Folger et al. (1997) use the same five strategies as Blake and Mouton's research of the 1960s and 1970s. Others have adapted these styles, as shown in the table below.

TABLE — CONFLICT STYLES

AUGSBURGER (1985)	CORMACK (1989)	LITTLEJOHN (2001)
1. flight	1. avoidance	1. avoidance
2. submission	2. defensiveness	
3. fight	3. attack	2. litigation
4. confrontation	4. confrontation	3. intervention
5. compromise	5. compromise	
6. negotiation		4. negotiation
7. competition		
8. collaboration		
		5. war

For several years I both used and taught these strategies, until an insightful workshop participant pointed out the violence inherent in them: at their core, they promote competition and winning and losing. In response to this comment, I designed nonviolent strategies, which we will explore next.

Conflict Resolution, Conflict Management

> *Out beyond ideas of wrongdoing and rightdoing*
> *there is a field.*
> *I will meet you there.*

Rumi

In developing nonviolent conflict strategies, I had to clarify my own views and bring them in line with our new story and a spirituality of nonviolence.

In my initial training in conflict, without any practical experience, I used the *etic* or "expert" lens. *Etic* theory and strategies are based on the theorist's worldview, culture, notions about conflict, and her or his inner conflicts. These may bear only some resemblance to the issues at hand, and need adapting to the lived reality of those in conflict. This *etic* approach lacks the perspective of the parties involved in the actual conflict.

Over many years of experience in the field, I have changed my *etic* lens for an *emic* lens. Doing so has helped me learn how to contextualize and adapt the theories, constructs and analyses to the lived reality of the people with whom I am working. I attempt to live from the inside out within the culture of the conflicted parties, which results in an *emic* analysis of the conflict.

In any discussion about conflict it is important to ensure that both the *emic* and *etic* approaches are present, adapting theory and practice accordingly when they no longer fit.

Conflict Resolution

When I began work in the conflict field, the focus was on conflict resolution strategies that would automatically take care of the differences between the parties. I remember learning in one conflict resolution training session about 40 ways to facilitate others' learning to deal with their conflicts!

The fact is that not every conflict can be resolved. Two obstacles to effective dispute resolution in hierarchical settings are, as Ury, Brett and Goldberg explain, "the organisation's highly centralized decision-making structure…and…the cultural background – the beliefs and practices – of the senior management, including the president … a culture stressing appearance of harmony, avoidance of confrontation and deference to authority."[2]

In the literature at the turn of the millennium, the approach became more nuanced, differentiating between conflict resolution in a broad sense and in a narrow sense, with strategies for each.

Kevin Avruch explains that conflict resolution in its broadest sense "refers to any strategy that brings a socially visible or public episode of conflict (a dispute) to an end...or even stops the violence."[3] Any tactic whose goal is simply an end to the conflict may be short-sighted, depending on the variables involved. When a conflict is deep-rooted or when there are power imbalances, gender issues or violence involved, it may simply be driven underground rather than resolved.

Genuine conflict resolution looks at strategies that go beyond the surface and examine the underlying causes. According to Avruch, "Resolution aims somehow to get to the root causes of a conflict and not merely treat its episodic or symptomatic manifestation, i.e. a particular dispute."[4]

Earlier, we explored deep-rooted or moral conflicts, based on identity, integrity, values and needs. Deep-rooted conflict falls into conflict resolution in the narrow sense, where the principals try to get to the underlying issues. Through dialogue, they choose to "develop and exercise a wide range of ways of relating to each other"[5] that both focuses and respects differences and similarities.

Conflict Management

Realizing over time that not all conflicts could be resolved, I began using the term *conflict management*. However, as conflict management became the "in" term, I found it was most often used synonymously, at least in the beginning, with *conflict resolution*.

Today, some researchers and practitioners make detailed distinctions between the two terms. We need both terms, but we need to redefine them. For deep-rooted conflicts, conflict management is a better term. These intractable conflicts cannot be resolved, but they can be managed with communication and mutual respect between the two conflicted parties. For conflicts that can have some resolution, especially where integrity and identity are not threatened, then conflict resolution is a more apt term. Currently, the two terms are inverted: *conflict resolution* is used for intractable conflicts, while *conflict management* is used for resolvable ones.

Conflict Transformation

> *Genuine transformation of conflict*
> *becomes possible*
> *when we move from blame to discovery.*
>
> Dean E. Peachy

Today, I use the term *conflict transformation* more because, as we know from our new story of home, conflict is energy, with both positive and negative potential ready for transformation. The term is also appearing in the more recent literature on conflict. In Carolyn Schrock-Shenk's words, "Conflict transformation…begins with and focuses more heavily on the people involved and on their relationships with each other…describing the essentially spiritual goals of conflict … 'love my neighbour as myself'."[6]

What is conflict transformation all about? After I realized that the game theory approach was not congruent with a spirituality of nonviolence and loving my enemy, I found a number of the conflict resolution and conflict management strategies to be very much focused on a win/lose model. More and more, I am coming to realize that nurturing a relationship in constructive and nonviolent ways is more important than winning and being right. Relearning which approaches work and when, recognizing that some work better than others, and realizing that some may need to be eliminated because of their intrinsic violence (e.g., competition and confrontation), I have developed an approach to conflict based on the values of our cosmic community and a spirituality of nonviolence explored in detail in Parts One and Two.

Throughout this book, I have mentioned my own conversion process regarding my theory and practice of handling conflict. Respecting how others approach conflict, I would like to introduce you to my journey of developing a model of dealing with conflict that better reflects quantum, organic principles and a spirituality of nonviolence. Two concrete differences in my model from others are obvious: my language when speaking about conflict, and the approaches used.

Previous linguistic and interpersonal communication studies have made me very sensitive to the nuances in language. I believe deeply that the language we use reveals our worldview, our cultures, our sex-role socialization and stereotyping. For this reason, in my own *kenosis* and *metanoia* (emptying out and conversion), I have let go of words and phrases often used to describe and understand conflict that I found violent, replacing them with nonviolent and empowering ones. The process continues as I integrate input from colleagues as well as workshop and course participants.

In the nonviolent approaches to conflict I have developed, I do not offer linear parameters, such as degrees of cooperation and assertiveness, nor do I focus on the goals or the relationship per se. Rather, my starting and ending point is transformation of conflict (and anger) energy. Because this energy is fluid, the repertoire I offer for transforming conflict is fluid: we can move from one approach to another to another, following the ebb and flow of the energy of two people dealing with their differences in interdependent, mutual, equal and reciprocal ways.

Nonviolent Repertoire

With quantum principles as the context of our new story of home, and the spirituality of nonviolence as both a way of life and a methodology, I now offer methods for transforming conflict based on what I have learned from the various theories and from my own life experience. These methods are used in a circular fashion, since different energy potentials meet interpersonal conflict energy potentials. They are presented in random order; none is better than or less violent than another. All are intended to be used nonviolently. All are intended to be cooperative and assertive. In any one conflict, I may use a number of these approaches. Channelling the energies that emerge as anger, fear, frustration and pain during the conflict into more constructive energies is the magic and the mystery of conflict transformation.

Each of the following five methods – which I call 5 Cs – focuses on the micro-transformation of self and other, which affects the macro picture of our cosmic home. Each is about emptying out what interferes with this transformation and the conversion that results. In naming these strategies, I have chosen words that honour the several ways the research indicates conflicts occur, but I move away from the game theory approach.

After a conflict, I reflect on it, pray about it, and pray for the other person or group involved. When I decide to meet with the other person about our problematic differences, I prepare my heart for the encounter. I have to process my emotions of anger, fear and hurt.

I am not suggesting a "head in the sand" approach in which I pray that the conflict will go away. Not at all. Rather, I pray for the nonviolent heart of flesh instead of the heart of stone (Ezekiel 36:26), and I use the abilities I have as a feeling and thinking being. Using "I" statements, I present the conflict issue from my perspective. Next, I detail each strategy and give an example of what it might look and sound like.

TABLE — 5 Cs: CONFLICT TRANSFORMATION: NONVIOLENT REPERTOIRE

1. Carefrontation
2. Coasting
3. Conciliation
4. Concession
5. Cooperation

---

1. Carefrontation

The meeting of two personalities is like the contact
of two chemical substances:
if there is any reaction, both are transformed.

Carl Jung

To avoid the negative connotations of *confrontation*, David Augsburger has coined the word *carefrontation*. This face-to-face listening-dialogue is both caring and challenging. "Carefronting is offering genuine care that bids another grow. Carefronting unites love and power ... concern for relationship with concern for goals. Carefronting is the way to communicate with both impact and respect, with truth and love."[7] Carefronting is loving, firm, centred, challenging, assertive and nonviolent.

Sometimes we have to deal with an issue because holding on to its energy in fear, anger or revenge blocks possibilities for growth and love. I know something is an issue for me by the intensity of emotion I experience or the amount of time I spend thinking about it, going over what I should have said and done. I know it is one that I need to deal with to release the energy tied up in it.

In these and other integrity-based situations, I use carefrontation. It is a case of "speaking the truth in love" (Ephesians 4:15) but the truth as I see it. Using "I" statements, I share the specific, concrete issue and how I feel about it; I "carefront" you. This does not mean that I control you; rather, I empower and free myself regardless of the outcome, which I do not control.

Example

In carefrontation, I use an "I" statement when sharing my hurt. "I was really hurt when you told me at the meeting today that I didn't know what I was talking about in the budget figures I gave. I spent a lot of time confirming these with the auditors and I would have appreciated if you had allowed me to finish giving the report before you made your comments." Using "I" statements allows me to share how I feel without attacking the other person.

2. Coasting

Coasting is a strategy I use when I am not ready to engage in the energy of a particular conflict. As the name suggests, when I coast, I choose to sidestep another person's energy for now. I do this for several reasons, including safety (physical, psychological and spiritual), importance of the issue at hand (not important at all or too important) and confidentiality (my role or the other's role).

When I coast, I respond to your story in ways that respect you and also respect and take care of me. Coasting is a way of saving energy and sidestepping a tough issue in a particular situation for a time, but it is not used to shirk responsibility indefinitely. My energy, for now, has limits.

Example

My noncommittal response in coasting respects the other but does not put me or my opinion out there. If I am in a violent domestic relationship and conflict occurs, I coast for self-protection. Or, I coast when I have a difference of opinion on an important issue but I sense my opinion cannot be heard. "That's certainly an interesting way of looking at capital punishment..." or "I see there are a number of options and you have presented one...."

3. Conciliation

Conciliation allows me to provide a space in which the other person's energy can be heard and blessed in a special way. I do this from an inner freedom and not a sense of guilt. For conciliation to transform both of our energies, it has to come from both: each of us listens and one of us acquiesces to the other's wishes.

Conciliation is not about saying "yes" when you mean "no." It is not about just pleasing the other. I have to be able to respond to your needs without becoming a doormat or a martyr.

Example

The following are typical conciliation statements:

"I would be happy to go to the movie you want to see, rather than the one I suggested."

"If you need the car this evening, I will be fine taking the bus."

"I would prefer to do the shopping on Saturday morning, but I can go along with Friday evening just as well."

"I don't see the situation that way, but I am willing to go along with the group."

4. Concession

Concession is mutual validation. The energy in a concession approach to conflict is focused on working toward meeting both sets of needs in some way. As each story is shared and each of us listens deeply, there comes a point in the dialogue where we can look at a settlement that meets each of our needs to a point. (This can occur when the issue is not based on the essence of our identity or integrity.) When this happens, the energy release of that particular conflict is more free-flowing.

Example

In a conflict over scarce resources, where each person needs the car at the same time but for different reasons, a concession could be this: "I am willing to do the grocery shopping with you first thing in the morning so I can use the car for my meeting at noon." For co-workers, it might be this: "I would be happy to change shifts with you so you can have the long weekend off."

5. Cooperation

Transforming the energies of conflicts related to our values, integrity and identity is the most challenging task in conflict transformation. It requires a fluid openness to stay with their energies for that eventual transformation. In these cases, the energy of each of us can become stalled and, at times, blocked with the focus on the other solely as the "enemy." Cooperation is a helpful strategy here.

When each of us is able to transcend our issues with a listening-dialogue that moves us beyond them, then we can cooperate to find a whole other reality. This reality both respects each person's concerns and invites us to move beyond them and live in true community. Cooperation, with its emphasis on using our energies for consensus and community, is about unconditional love.

Example

What may start out as coasting in a particular conflict may become cooperation as the listening-dialogue ebbs and flows in nonviolent ways. By listening to a colleague's point of view, I can find a way to achieve a common goal: "Oh, so what you mean by equality in the workplace is…." I move from my coasting approach to a cooperation stance as the issues evolve, and the discussion deepens in a respectful way.

The 5 Cs of conflict transformation – carefrontation, coasting, conciliation, concession and cooperation – are based on quantum principles, a spirituality of nonviolence and listening-dialogue. Each story is heard deeply and responded to, using a nonblaming, nonviolent approach.

Each of these methods, and any combination of them, can be used in the escalation, climax and de-escalation of any conflict. To demonstrate how these strategies move from one to another in a given conflict, I share the following example from my own life.

"I Knew You'd Come!"

Working as a speech-language pathologist for many years meant travelling to dozens of schools. On one occasion, a friend commented in front of a large group that it must be great driving around to 49 schools and enjoying myself. I had worked hard to train as a therapist and then worked even harder to get the service into the schools. I was very hurt at what I saw as criticism of me and my "easy" job.

I said nothing at the time (coasting), but I knew I would have to approach the other person about it (carefront) in a different setting and at another time. However, it took me a number of weeks to prepare my mind and heart for this listening-dialogue. I had to deal with my desire to even the score. Finally, when the time arrived to talk about the incident, the other person said to me, "I knew you'd come!"

I felt an urge to respond in kind, but because I had taken the time to prepare from the inside out, I was able to stay grounded. Then, in carefrontation, I shared my hurt in light of the difficult journey I had had in my organization in becoming a speech-language pathologist. My friend listened attentively and, from there, we were able to move together to a cooperative focus on the conflict and the resulting transformation in our relationship.

Let's take a closer look at a communication skill that is key to the process: listening-dialogue.

Listening-Dialogue

*Listening well is at the heart of intimacy
and connection.*

Harriet Goldhor Lerner

The Essence of Dialogue

Dialogue is not just about speaking; it is also about silence and listening. Dialogue means interaction, subject to subject. It is not a series of monologues in which each person, subtly or otherwise, informs, corrects and straightens out the other. Rather, it is about two people taking turns listening and responding, building on each other's expressed thoughts and feelings.

Dialogue is not a win/lose exercise. Instead, it is a face-to-face sharing of the differences that have become issues between us. We stay in this fluid movement of listening and dialogue without interrupting the other, for as long as we are able to and need to, so we can come to some deep place of being and knowing our own and each other's stories. Thus, says Joseph Phelps, dialogue is "a way of thinking, seeing, hearing, relating to, and...talking with our 'enemies.'"[8] We become the subjects of our own and each other's transformation, and as Phelps adds, "the goal is changed from conquering to growing, from silencing to knowing, from telling to asking."[9]

With qualities of faith, hope, love and humility, dialogue is about the sacred Word between us. "To speak a true word is to transform the world," suggests human rights educator Paulo Friere.[10] Because of its interdependent and reciprocal nature, dialogue is founded on love. It is as close to that agapic, unconditional love as we can get.

Dialogue also challenges us to assert deep faith in the other person, even in the midst of the conflict. Hope, along with faith and love, is the essence of dialogue because it points to the "not yet" in our incompleteness.

Dialogue pushes each of us to hone our deepest convictions as well as critique our underlying assumptions about this conflict. The magic of true dialogue is that it is interdependent, reciprocal, equal and mutual. Each person influences the other in an ebb and flow that cannot be scripted beforehand. The energies of each co-mingle and create something new.

Listening-dialogue enfleshes organic/holistic quantum principles. By actively listening during the conflict, we can catch what is unsaid beneath all that is said. This type of listening requires us to wait and do nothing for a time. With silence, the inner clutter, noise of right answers and brilliant retorts are stilled to create an open stance for receiving the other's story. Bestselling author and therapist Harriet Goldhor Lerner tells us, "We all are capable of much deeper levels of listening than we may ever tap into. Compassion, connection, detachment and appreciation for the sacred come together in this pure moment of listening and unconditional love."[11]

The ebb and flow of listening-dialogue allows for each story to be shared and listened to from deep within. I am challenged to quell my desire to interrupt the other with the proverbial red flag word "but," which I want to use to correct, inform, teach, deny or negate what the other person is saying. Listening-dialogue is an interactive process that, as Ronald Fisher notes, "promotes collaborative conflict analysis and problem solving…that addresses basic human needs and promotes the building of peace, justice and equality."[12]

Communion

*Love...is the foundation of dialogue
and dialogue itself.*

Paulo Freire

Pruning

In a dialogue, I help transform the energy of a conflict when I give the other person the opportunity to share her or his story, when I am disposed to deep, active listening in the listening-dialogue flow. "In problem-solving through dialogue, the process is less structured," explains Deborah Kolb. "Goals emerge through mutual inquiry...flexible and adaptive rather than controlling in response to uncertainty."[13] In nature, pruning is the process of getting rid of whatever prevents new growth and life. Similarly, pruning is getting rid of those aspects of my agenda that prevent your growth. As I listen to you, I listen with a heart of flesh rather than a heart of stone (Ezekiel 36:26). I create a sacred space for the other in which she or he feels accepted just for being. I prune my heart, mind and spirit from the old story – those attitudes and actions that speak of violence, power over, dominating and winning. As a result, I am grafted onto the new story.

Communion

When we get to the point in the conflict where we are looking at both sets of needs and are moving closer to conflict transformation, we build bridges through communication. Indeed, communication and communion are connected; both are about union. Communication experts Pearce and Littlejohn state that "Communication then, is not merely a process of transmitting information to another person; it is always a continuing process of coordinating actions."[14] Joseph Phelps adds, it is "communion in which we are mutually informed, purified, illumined, and reunited to ourselves, to one another and to God."[15]

This is not to say that in our communication everything will be fully resolved. Rather, no matter the outcome (which at times may be a break in the relationship, such as divorce), the listening-dialogue has brought about a conclusion in nonviolent ways.

It takes a great deal of trial and error to be able, through self-knowledge and self-acceptance, to recognize our own violent tendencies and to be able to move to nonviolence. As Eggleton and Trafford remind us, "It is the way that we respond to conflict which determines whether the outcome of that conflict is creative and healthy, or limiting and unhealthy."[16]

Who Owns the Conflict?

In the end, terms and theories do not make conflict disappear in our lives. Conflict is here to stay, so who owns it? There are several possible answers. We often see others as the cause of the conflict. Or we accept all the fault ourselves, which is rarely appropriate. But for anything constructive and nonviolent to happen with this conflict, both parties must take responsibility for the conflict. Otherwise, we get into the games of moves and countermoves, and ultimately win and lose. To sum up, we can look at this issue in one of four ways, as shown in the following table.

TABLE — WHO OWNS THE CONFLICT?

1. **No** conflict.
2. **You** own the conflict.
3. **I** own the conflict.
4. **We** own the conflict.

7

MEDIATION

Mediators do not make decisions for parties....

Karl A. Slaikeu

Parameters of Mediation

A resource book on conflict and anger would be incomplete without at least a cursory look at mediation, which more and more people in conflict are using.

Mediation (from the Latin *medius,* in the middle) began with disputes in labour management. A third-party mediator, the one in the middle, would work with the two sides to help them reach a settlement. Mediation was later adopted by business organizations. Numerous theories and approaches to mediation as a way to diminish the costs of organizational conflicts became integral to business training programs.

Because of lengthy delays in having legal cases heard, mediation was next adopted as an alternative to the court system. It became one of the main aspects of Alternative Dispute Resolution (ADR), whose purported goals were to give the disputants more control over the outcomes of their conflicts, reduce waiting and settlement times, and alleviate people's fear and stress around going to court.[1]

It is not known whether mediation has achieved these goals, but it is a step in the right direction: each party must agree both to the mediation process and to the choice of mediator, and the process is designed so that the parties are in each other's presence in a safe and nonviolent environment. In this way, they can listen to each other and be open to working out their differences in mutually accommodating ways.

Mediation is part of the game theory approach to conflict. It is based on negotiation, but features more finely tuned bargaining and persuasion. As Ury, Brett and Goldberg explain in *Getting Disputes Resolved*, "Mediation is negotiation often assisted by a third party. A mediator can help parties move past a deadlock over positions by getting them to identify their underlying interests and develop creative solutions that satisfy those interests."[2] Mediation can be effective when parties are unable to work out solutions on their own.

Arbitration is a particular type of mediation. Here the mediator is given the power – by the labour union, the organization or the government involved – to listen to the disputants' stories and the issues of conflict and then impose a binding solution (binding arbitration).

The Mediator

The mediator must be properly trained and have an intuitive sense of the ebb and flow of the process. She or he is supposed to be impartial and nonjudgmental. As a neutral outsider, the mediator strives to be a bridge-builder, helping the principals move from entrenched positions to more open communication and mutual understanding.

Qualities of a competent mediator include objectivity, good listening skills, awareness of one's own biases, assertiveness, strong communication skills, and sensitivity to disputants' feelings. Mediators must be realistic about the limitations of mediation and of their own abilities in this area.

The mediator engages both parties in impartial ways. Because the mediator comes to the process with her or his own inner conflicts, sex-role biases and stereotypes from the cultures to which she or he belongs, ensuring impartiality in this role is key.

The role of the mediator is to provide a safe, accepting and peaceful space in which the disputants can hear each other and look at ways of exploring the conflict, with the aid of the mediator's impartial presence. This means that the mediator does not give advice to the parties or solve the disputants' problem, either as a therapist or as a counsellor. Nor is the mediator there as a lawyer, even though many lawyers are now involved in ADR and mediation. In other words, the mediator is a facilitator, not a negotiator or arbitrator; it is not her or his role to come up with a solution to the conflict but, rather, to provide a safe space where the disputants, in respect and nonviolence, can determine a common ground that accommodates the needs of both parties.

Co-mediation has become popular recently for the same reasons that co-facilitation has: it allows the second mediator to use eyes, ears, heart and intuition to support the lead mediator. Co-mediators can also give each other feedback on impartiality, fairness, pressure, persuasion and progress.

Types of Mediation

Only certain types of conflicts lend themselves to mediation. The more tangible and the more concrete the conflict issues, the better the chances of finding some common ground in mediation.

When I first trained in mediation and, later, taught and facilitated the process, the focus was on a universal way of mediating, seemingly good for all situations. The more recent literature now explores different types of mediation, including the prescriptive model, the active/passive model and the elicitive model.

Prescriptive Model

The *prescriptive model* (also known as the directive or bargaining model) is more the *etic* or expert approach to mediation. As with bargaining, it is directive and controlling, with the mediator using a four-step model of mediation, no matter what issues, cultures or parties are involved. A summary of the process follows:

Step One

Here, the mediator sets the stage, introduces the process and the parties with the following sequence:

1. Greet the parties warmly and help them feel comfortable.

2. Introduce yourself, your training, and state the purpose of the meeting.

3. Describe your role as mediator.

4. Review the guidelines for being together: no interrupting; no name-calling, cursing, abuse.

5. Stress confidentiality and your notetaking to be used solely for the purposes of chronicling issues and events.

6. Explain the process.

7. Obtain consent to proceed.

Step Two

In this step, the mediator directs the parties to identify the problem in a movement from positions to underlying issues, wants and needs. Here, each person tells her or his story: both the facts and the emotions experienced. The mediator's role is to facilitate this process.

1. Invite one party to tell his or her side of the story (5 to 7 minutes maximum). The first speaker may be the one who requested the mediation or the one who appears to be in the most distress. Another option is to flip a coin or choose any other way that can equalize power regarding sex, age, status and other factors.

2. Restate the facts and reflect the feelings. The mediator does this in a minute or less, ensuring no assumptions are made by checking things out with the speaker.

3. Invite the second party to tell her or his story.

4. Restate the facts and reflect the feelings.

Step Three

In Step Three, the mediator facilitates the parties' brainstorming for possible solutions (problem solving).

1. Summarize and review both sets of facts and feelings.

2. Highlight the common areas.

3. Request comments from the parties regarding "new" information heard.

4. Redirect the parties to talk to each other now instead of to you.

5. Reflect any intense feelings and restate any facts pertinent to the problem solving.

6. Invite the parties to brainstorm for possible solutions.

7. Facilitate the parties' choosing two or three solutions they could live with.

8. Look at the consequences of each solution for each party.

9. Move the parties to one concrete solution that is agreeable and satisfactory to both.

Step Four

The mediator helps the parties make the agreed-upon solution concrete using a written agreement signed by both, with the mediator as witness.

1. Write down the solution the parties have agreed to, using a mediation agreement form.

2. Be specific and concrete regarding which party does what, where, when, why and how. Avoid ambiguities and judgments like "later," "fair," etc.

3. Ensure both parties agree to the wording.

4. Sign the agreement (both parties and mediator as witness) to confirm the commitment made.

5. Congratulate the parties on their sincerity and hard work.

This model may work in certain situations, and participants may feel empowered as they learn more life-giving ways for dealing with conflict. But when mediators see conflict solely as problem solving, they are unlikely to get beneath the problem to the parties' underlying cultural mores and values. The danger in the prescriptive model is that middle-class North American assumptions about conflict and third-party roles may become the definitive word on the subject.

Active/Passive Mediation

Is the settlement of a dispute the result of the mediator's input, or is it due to what happens between the disputants? Most of the literature insists on the mediator being a neutral third party whose role is to provide a safe environment in which the disputants can settle the conflict themselves. When the mediator is there solely as an assuring presence, then it is *passive mediation*.

When, on the other hand, the mediator offers a substantive contribution to the settlement, this is *active mediation*. (Many would not consider this latter sense true mediation, seeing it more as adjudication or arbitration.) In the active model, the "neutral" outsider listens to the evidence and judges (adjudicates) a particular settlement for the parties to consider. As an arbitrator, the outsider arbitrates or imposes the solution that binds the parties.

Elicitive Model

The *elicitive model* highlights the *emic* or contextualized approach to problem solving. Here the third party learns to listen to the issues from within the culture itself. It aims to discover the models that emerge from the resources present in a particular setting and respond to the needs in that context. This model is similar to the andragogical (adult learning) processes used by Paulo Freire (1987) and Jane Vella (1994). The mediator is a supportive, safe presence while the principals involved determine the techniques and strategies needed. Some mediators are moving more to the elicitive passive model, which is less directive and more empowering.[3] In adult learning, the learner is an equal partner with the teacher. Vella suggests effective adult learning and teaching are person-centred, part of the whole of the person's life.[4] Freire considers dialogue the methodology of adult learning.[5]

Risks of Mediation

Mediation is a resource to be used ethically and with care. The mediator must be alert to her or his own partiality to one or other of the parties, resulting in a subtle power over and power imbalance for the other party. If mediation is used too soon, and too readily, it may prevent the parties from dealing with the issues themselves. It can create a dependency (and lower self-esteem) in participants who tend to seek outside help to "fix" things. Finally, it may result in surface changes within the session but with no tangible results outside the session.

Interactive Conflict Resolution: An Alternative to Mediation

Canadian researcher Ronald Fisher's work on Interactive Conflict Resolution (ICR), although not designed as mediation per se, has some useful premises that could apply to mediation. Fisher's ICR approach to conflict, based on his own research and work in the area of international conflicts, involves "small-group problem solving discussion between unofficial representatives of identity groups or states involved in destructive conflict…. It is facilitated face-to-face activities in communication…that promote collaborative conflict analysis and problem solving…that address basic human needs, and promotes the building of peace, justice and equality."[6] This approach could be useful when there is a stalemate in passive mediation, for example. It could allow the mediator to facilitate the process more actively, with the consent of both parties, setting up unofficial problem-solving meetings with each party outside the mediation, so that when the principals return to mediation, more common ground is accessible. This may be the final step that averts the parties from going to court over the issue, where it will become a win/lose situation.

The Benefits of Conflict

> *Difference of opinion leads to inquiry,*
> *and inquiry to truth.*
>
> Thomas Jefferson

Conflict serves a purpose in our lives, and indeed has numerous benefits. These benefits pertain to both intrapersonal and interpersonal conflicts, given the interconnectedness and interdependence between the two.

Conflict Offers a Catalyst for Growth

When we see conflict as negative, unnatural or pathological, we will not find any benefits. When, on the other hand, we view conflict as an inherent and natural part of our daily interactions, then we can approach it more positively, aware of its tremendous potential for bringing about growth and transformation. Conflict nudges us out of our complacency into chaos and disorder, the catalyst for new growth. That time of chaos is a golden opportunity to look at how new ways of doing things might enhance our interpersonal relationships.

Conflict is an occasion to deepen a given relationship, where both parties share responsibility for what is happening. Lewis Coser takes this point a step further, saying that "Often conflict is necessary to maintain relationships."[7]

In some cases, a function of conflict may be to terminate the relationship. Even though not all conflicts can be resolved, all can be opportunities for transformation. Dealing nonviolently and proactively with conflict does not necessarily mean "living happily ever after," but even when we cannot continue in relationship, transforming this interpersonal conflict in a spirituality of nonviolence can still happen.

Conflict Increases Our Self-Knowledge

Interpersonal conflicts can also be the occasion to look at one's identity – both intrapersonal and interpersonal – in a particular group. Conflict is necessary in "establishing and maintaining the identity and boundary lines of societies and groups," adds Lewis Coser.[8] For those who do not have a clear sense of who they are as separate from another (such as women who have been socialized to know themselves only as someone's daughter, wife, mother or partner), conflict can clarify identity and strengthen or redefine relationships.

Conflict Grounds Us in Gaia

Conflict energy connects us to the transformative energy in our cosmic community of Gaia. It reminds us of our fluid interdependence and interconnectedness with all of life.

PART III: REFLECTION AND DISCUSSION STARTERS

1. What have you learned about conflict from home, church, society? Is it a more negative or a more positive thing? Why?

2. How do your intrapersonal conflicts affect your interpersonal conflicts?

3. Conflict has its own ebb and flow. Has exploring the stages of conflict helped you understand it better? How?

4. Do you see conflict as just a problem to be solved? Why or why not?

5. Culture, stress, self-esteem, power, gender and personality are some of the variables affecting conflict. Which variable(s) do you need to attend to more in your conflicts? Why? How can you do this?

6. The storming or conflict stage is a natural part of group development and the crux of the group's life. Do you agree? Why or why not?

7. "Who owns the conflict?" can be helpful in transforming interpersonal conflicts. How? Why?

8. Is the game theory approach to conflict helpful or unhelpful for you? Explain.

9. Conflict transformation, with its nonviolent repertoire (the 5 Cs), is based on our new story of home and quantum principles. Discuss these connections at both the intrapersonal and interpersonal levels.

10. Listening-dialogue and communion are integral to cosmic conflict transformation. Discuss.

11. What have you learned about the reasons for and risks of mediation?

12. What are two or three benefits of conflict as normal, natural and necessary in your life?

PART IV

ANGER AS COMMUNICATION

8

THE EMOTION OF ANGER

Emotions are really what conflict is all about.

Wendy Grant

Part III of this resource book provided an overview of the complexity of intra-personal and interpersonal conflict, a repertoire of nonviolent ways to transform its cosmic energy. Part IV examines what unhealthy anger looks like and sounds like – physically, psychologically and spiritually.

Cosmic Energy of Emotions

What Is an Emotion?

In my experience, organizations tend to overlook or ignore people's emotions, even when these are palpable and the result is passive-aggressive behaviour. In our new story, emotions are part of the cosmic energy available to us for transformation.

An emotion is a complex pattern involving all body systems: physiological changes, expressive reactions and subjective feelings.[1] According to Williard Gaylin, author of *The Rage Within*, "An emotion is a complex phenomenon with at least three separate elements: one autonomic, one a function of the central nervous system and one cognitive."[2]

Two nervous systems regulate our bodies: the parasympathetic and the sympathetic. The parasympathetic regulates such everyday activities as digestion and recuperative processes, while the sympathetic (or autonomic) system prepares the body for arousal when needed.

Physiology of Emotions

When you experience fear, love or anger, how does your body respond? The range of physiological changes includes an increased amount of cortisol and adrenaline (flight) and nor-adrenaline (fight) into the bloodstream. The resulting changes in the body consist of dilation or constriction of the pupils, increased heart rate, sweaty palms, controlled or released sphincters, redirection of the blood from one part of the body to another (as in cold hands and feet) and flushed or pale face and ears. As Carl Georg Lange and William James, editors of *The Emotions*, stress, "We have in every emotion…sure and tangible factors: a cause – a sensory impression which usually is modified by memory or a previous associated image, an effect … namely vaso-motor changes and consequent changes in bodily and mental functions."[3]

We may use the words *emotions* and *feelings* interchangeably, but they mean different things. Emotions are primarily psychological experiences, while feelings are the physical experiences that interpret the emotions. Williard Gaylin explains,

> feelings are mushy, difficult, non-palpable slippery things even by definition … they are that elusive, neglected aspect of emotions. Obviously, in addition to the autonomic responses…the feeling of the emotion comes through. We feel. The feeling then allows us to utilize our intelligence and rationality when available…to make a decision (about our response)…. Feelings become guides…. They are a form of fine-tuning, directing the ways in which we will manipulate our environment.[4]

Feelings help us interpret our emotions so we can respond by making judgments and choices. All emotions have bodily feelings that help us translate what is going on, but not all feelings (such hunger or sleepiness) are emotions.

Rationality of Emotions

How can emotions be considered rational? Yet Carol Tavris concludes that anger is a rational emotion, involving judgment and choice.[5] Because the body's physiological response tends to be the same for all emotions, the rational part of our emotional response is our ability to specify which emotion(s) we are experiencing in a given situation. In other words, a human emotion, because of this interpretive component, is different from a basic stimulus-response instinct or reflex, such as pulling my hand away from a hot stove.

Classifications of Emotions

Can you name some positive emotions? What about negative ones? From our dualistic training, we may be more aware of so-called negative emotions, such as anger, shame, hate and fear, and try to avoid or deny them because we have been taught to see them as bad or sinful. But, explains Susan Balfour in her book *Managing Stress in a Changing World*, "These feelings are perfectly legitimate, and it is in denying them or being ashamed of them that we do ourselves damage."[6]

Emotions are also classified as primary or secondary. A primary emotion is one that is basic to other emotions: examples include fear, embarrassment, frustration, grief, rejection and shame. Anger, meanwhile, is considered to be a secondary emotion: a primary emotion lies underneath it.

Yet another classification involves nine major emotions and their interrelationships: interest, enjoyment, surprise, distress, anger, shame, guilt, fear and contempt. Fear, distress, anger, shyness and guilt can be aspects of anxiety.[7]

A final classification of emotions is the container idea, which may be more prevalent in North America. This theory sees emotions as all bottled up within us (e.g., "full of anger," "boiling over," "letting off steam," "holding it in"). We (the container) become too full at times, causing us to overflow or "explode."

Emotions are neither good nor bad, positive nor negative. Rather they are part of the cosmic energy of our universe, at times placid and calm, at others, wild and generative. All are God-given and we need each of them in order to be whole. Our challenge is to befriend their energies in the depths of our beings. Although exploring the energies of all our emotions would prove fruitful, the focus herein is anger. The rest of Part IV details our unhealthy anger expression, as an exercise in consciousness-raising for learning healthy anger communication in Part V.

The Red in the Rainbow: The Colours of Anger

> *The taboos against feeling*
> *and expressing anger are…powerful.*
>
> Harriet Goldhor Lerner

What colour is anger for you? Do you "see red" when you're angry? In one anger management training program, I invited the participants to discover, in small groups, what they had learned about anger from home, school, church and society. I suggested that they find symbols for these insights. One group drew a rainbow minus the red. These participants had been taught to experience the rainbow of life but suppress their anger. "Unfortunately," says Nathaniel Branden in *A Woman's Self-esteem*, "when we were growing up, no one ever told us how to handle anger. Often, the implication was that if we were a good person, we would never experience it, let alone express it."[8]

Metaphorically, anger has many colours, including red, which is that flash of healthy anger. Purple represents congested, inhibited anger that we internalize and leave unexpressed. Blue is anger turned inward in self-blame and low self-esteem, which becomes depression. Black is destructive, aggressive anger, while white is a cold, calculating desire to annihilate the object of our anger.[9]

It is crucial that we accept and welcome anger into our lives. The challenge is to be angry and, at the same time, be aware. Like conflict, anger is a gift of energy that is integral to our well-being, but one that is neither understood nor appreciated. "Anger is a signal and one worth listening to," Harriet Goldhor Lerner reminds us, "...a message that we are being hurt, our rights are being violated, that our needs or wants are not being adequately met or simply that something is not right."[10] Although we all experience this wonderful and challenging energy, we misunderstand its necessity and usefulness. For this reason, we try to deny, suppress or get rid of it. We find it difficult to embrace its energy and to learn how to express it in healthy, constructive and nonviolent ways.

We will focus here on our intrapersonal and interpersonal anger, both of which are integral to who we are. Anger related to systemic injustices, international violence and oppression, though equally important, is beyond the scope of these pages.

Be Angry and Be Aware

When we believe that all our emotions are God-given, that they are energy potential challenging us to growth and transformation, then each one "exists for a reason and always deserves our respect and attention," as Lerner puts it.[11] The Christian scripture passage "Be angry but sin not" (Ephesians 4:26) summarizes my position on anger. Anger is a God-given emotion for our protection, but we must use its powerful energy with full awareness. Being aware means respecting our anger and using it in nonviolent and constructive ways, with ourselves and with others.

Anger Variables

Anger is a socially constructed experience.

H. Kassinove & D.G. Sukhodolsky

Anger and Culture

From a scientific perspective, the physiological changes that occur in the body when we are angry can be tracked and are the same across cultures, yet each culture determines how these reactions are labelled, understood and acted out.

Some emotions may not even exist in certain cultures. For example, in one Canadian Inuit culture, there are no situations that justify anger. Because they live their lives with more emphasis on the group rather than the individual, people of this culture deal with conflict and anger in ways quite different from most North Americans. The latter, with a greater focus on individualism, tend to "move against" (be angry at) or move away (withdraw) from people and situations rather than "move with," as in the Inuit culture.

Anger and Gender

Men's angry outbursts are usually accepted
by other men and soothed by women.

Marcia Starck and Gwen Stern

Our North American culture, based on a dualistic worldview of subject-object, attributes anger differently to men and women. A great number of men, trained to be dominant, have been taught to externalize their anger in aggressive and violent ways. A large proportion of North American women, meanwhile, have been socialized to see their expression of anger as bad and even destructive. From infancy onwards, women have been taught that anger in females is unfeminine, unladylike and sexually unattractive. Women who express their anger overtly, constructively and nonviolently are in the minority.

Anger and Aggression

> "A Poison Tree"
> I was angry with my friend:
> I told my wrath, my wrath did end.
> I was angry with my foe:
> I told it not, my wrath did grow.
>
> William Blake

Aggression's primary focus is on physical harm of the other, while the term *violence,* as used herein, refers more broadly to psychological and spiritual harm as well. Although our physiology provides us with the physical means to become both aggressive and angry, it is a learned choice. The long debate about the innateness of aggression and ancillary violence prompted the American Psychological Association to review all of the research related to aggression and violence. Here is its conclusion: "We are not genetically predisposed to violence ... [it is] more "the product of human culture, ... social learning."[12] Today, we recognize that we can unlearn this behaviour.

Despite such findings, why is the North American culture increasingly turning to aggression and violence to deal with differences? In fact, it has been suggested that unhealthy anger has reached epidemic proportions, as noted in the all too frequent incidents of domestic violence and rape.

Does expressing anger automatically lead to violence and aggression? No. Just as we choose to get angry, we can choose how to express anger. As Richard Gregg, author of *The Power of Nonviolence*, points out, "Anger as well as love, can be creative for both are expressions or modes of energy."[13]

A nonviolent expression of anger is possible, and indeed is integral to a life imbued with a spirituality of nonviolence. Learning how to be nonviolent is a lifelong process, as Gandhi and other prophets of nonviolence remind us.

Anger and Personality

> *The childhood shows the [hu]man,*
> *as morning shows the day.*
>
> John Milton

Our basic temperament or personality is a combination of nature and nurture. Our genetic makeup inclines us toward being more extroverted than introverted, more logical and scientific than imaginative and artistic. Then, through the nurturing of our early years, when we learned to get our basic needs met through certain behaviours, our own particular personality evolved. We fine-tune certain traits in a combination that makes us who we are. Anger follows a similar evolution. It is suggested that during these formative years, through an osmosis process of trial and error, "our basic patterns in relation to anger are formed."[14]

Over 2400 years ago, Hippocrates proposed four temperament types: sanguine, choleric, melancholic and phlegmatic. People of sanguine temperament are extroverted and friendly but can be disorganized, insecure and fearful. Those of choleric temperament are also extroverted but rather strong willed, hot-tempered and self-sufficient. People of melancholic temperament are more introverted; they are perfectionists and the most talented and creative of the four types. Those who have a phlegmatic temperament are highly introverted and are more passive.

Two instruments for discerning personality

Today, two commonly used assessments help us discern our personality: the Myers-Briggs Personality Inventory and the Enneagram.

1. Myers-Briggs Personality Inventory

The Myers-Briggs Personality Inventory is based on four Jungian constructs about how we are in the world. Our personality type can shed some light on how we relate to anger in our lives. Assessment tests and analyses of this Inventory are available in most places. Your results will be a particular combination of the four functions (for example, INTJ):

1) Extrovert or Introvert (E or I): Outer world or inner world

2) Sensing or Intuiting (S or N): Information gathering

3) Thinking or Feeling (T or F): Problem solving

4) Judging or Perceiving (J or P): Decision making

2. The Enneagram

From the Greek *ennea,* meaning nine, the Enneagram is a theory of personality based on nine compulsions. Once we determine our major compulsion, our goal is conversion. The enneagram approaches the personality from three centres. These are depicted in order from 1 to 9 around a circle. We live primarily from one of these centres: the "gut" (numbers 8, 9, 1), the "heart" (numbers 2, 3, 4) and the "head" (5, 6, 7). Each number in each of the three centres has nuances, which explore the different compulsions.

*

Personality inventories and constructs can help each of us know ourselves better, but they are not intended to label and judge people, a subtle form of violence. If anyone asks you your letters or number without there being a trusting relationship and a context for deepening the relationship (Myers-Briggs was designed to see whether two people might be compatible in the intimacy of a marriage), then I suggest you respond with some "coasting" response: "Oh, on a given day, I could be any one or all of them!"

Over the course of our lives, the results from these personality indicators can shift somewhat. Books and courses on the Myers-Briggs Personality Inventory and the Enneagram are widely available.

9

WHAT IS ANGER?

*Emotions are always involved in conflicts
and one of the most common is anger.*

David Johnson

Charles Darwin, who studied what he called anger in animals and then extrapo-lated from his findings to humans, is the author of the *biological approach*. Seeing a stimulus-response reflex in animals, Darwin defined anger as a survival instinct, a biological reflex with a dualistic response of fight or flight.

The essence of anger became distorted when Darwin concluded that it was synonymous with rage and aggression. Carol Tavris explains, "By lumping these three feelings together, however, Darwin severely restricted his analysis, for he was led to conclude that anger, like rage, is solely a response to threat and danger and that anger, like rage, implies an instinctive aggressive behaviour."[1]

Seen from this biological perspective, anger is an emotion coming from a frustra-tion-expression-action. What this means is there is a build-up of energy; we act out of this energy, destroying whatever frustrates us; we hit, pound, hurt or kill. With the cause of our distress eliminated, we experience momentary release from the unbearable physical tension.

The *frustration-aggression approach* to anger is similar. When we are frustrated, says Magda Arnold, author of *Emotion and Personality*, anger is seen as a "reaction to something that does harm here and now."[2] Both of these approaches assume that anger is uncontrollable and must be released and expressed.

Sigmund Freud first explored the *psychoanalytic approach*. In the development of his psychoanalytic theory, Freud's concept of the unconscious suggests that many people repress their emotions, including anger, storing them in the unconscious, where they continue to cause harm. These emotions are not consciously recognized, accepted and dealt with. Anger, from this perspective, becomes dangerous.

The biological and psychoanalytic perspectives have evolved over time, but many of us may still see anger as innate aggression. According to Tavris, the following misconceptions still surface:

TABLE — MISCONCEPTIONS ABOUT ANGER

* Anger and aggression are inextricably, biologically linked; anger is the feeling and aggression its overt expression; but both are aspects of the aggressive instinct.
* Anger is the instinctive response to threat and to the frustration of your goals and desires.
* If the outward expression of anger is blocked, anger turns inward and you feel it as depression, guilt, shame, anxiety or lethargy.[3]

The current psychoanalytic approach suggests that emotions determine our thinking and behaviour. In other words, we cannot experience an emotion that is disconnected from similar feelings of that emotion in the past.

The *behaviourist perspective* (remember Pavlov's dogs and Skinner's regimen of rewards and punishments based on the sequence of stimulus, response, reinforcement?) regarding anger is based on the idea that all behaviour is learned through trial and error. When force gets results, then the action is repeated; when punishment follows, then the action is not repeated.

The *cognitive approach* to anger focuses on our thinking and how it affects our feelings and behaviours. Cognitive psychologists believe that the nature of thinking heavily influences the emotions that we feel and it is these emotions which then drive our behaviour, say the authors of *Anger Management: A Practical Guide.* "Nothing makes us angry in reality. It is we ourselves who make us so by interpreting what happens to us as an attack on us as being unjustified, unfair. The moment we *interpret* something as hostile, we become physiologically aroused."[4]

Aaron Beck and Albert Ellis are two theorists associated with this approach. Beck suggests our "distorted thinking" leads to certain negative behaviours. Ellis maintains that our "irrational beliefs" move us to angry behaviours; his rational emotive therapy focuses on changing these beliefs.

Definitions of Anger

> *Point not at others' spots with a foul finger.*
>
> Proverb

A Curse or a Blessing?

The following definitions of anger are differentiated primarily into two types:

* destructive anger, uncontrollable and therefore to be suppressed; and

* constructive anger, a human emotion under our conscious control, and therefore a human blessing.

Let's begin with James Averill's definition of anger, one of the most frequently cited texts on the many and varied aspects of anger.

> Anger [is] a conflictive emotion, that on the biological level is related to aggressive systems, and even more important to the capacities for cooperative and social living, symbolization and reflective self-awareness, that on the psychological level, is aimed at the correction of some appraised wrong and that on the socio-cultural level, functions to uphold accepted standards of conduct.[5]

Other definitions from various disciplines highlight several aspects of its complexity. Anger is related to uneasiness, hurt, frustration and rejection, and is the conscious response to injustice, loss or grievance.[6] Anger is a potential source of mobilization for action against an injustice one has experienced.[7] Anger is an emotional response to provocation.[8] Anger is a reaction to a hurt or loss.[9] Anger is a legitimate feeling that can be expressed in both healthy and unhealthy ways.[10] Anger is connected with feelings of irritation because of the thwarting of some desire or expectation.[11]

I define interpersonal anger as a holistic physiological, psychological and spiritual response to a perceived personal or social hurt or injustice. Including a spiritual component makes the definition broader for a number of reasons. After all, anger is a God-given emotion, and my experiences of anger affect my spiritual life.

Like conflict, anger can be both intrapersonal and interpersonal. Intrapersonal anger is a distress signal: I am angry with myself because there is a gap between what I believe and what I do. Awareness of our intrapersonal anger is important, because it is part of our journey to integration and transformation. By facing my inner anger in gentleness and love, I recognize that this anger is normal.

Causes of Anger

Perception is more powerful than fact.

Joan Chittister

The causes of our anger include perceived hurt, physical, psychological and spiritual harm, unmet needs and expectations, violation of rights, attack on our self-esteem, and rejection. (Note the emphasis on *perceived*.) It is crucial to put this range of causes into perspective, or it might seem that we have reason to be angry all the time. Carol Tavris stresses, "Anger is not an inevitable consequence of arousal but an acquired one. It means that anger is generated and reduced by how we interpret the world and the events that happen to us."[12] Like conflict, anger energy is latent, with its own ebb and flow, depending on our body chemistry, temperament, self-esteem, frustration threshold, intrapersonal conflicts, life experiences and expectations in our relationships. The authors of *Anger Management* point out, "We are influenced not only by our families but by the way relatives, friends, co-workers, authority figures and strangers deal with their anger. After many personal experiences with anger, we develop our own style of displaying and hiding anger."[13]

The most common stimuli of our anger are those people with whom we have some type of intimacy in both interdependent and dependent relationships. For most of us, anger occurs in our relationships with family, spouse, siblings, partners, friends and others connected to us in ongoing and important ways. Circumstances and events that matter to us also become potential stimuli for our anger.

Another source of our anger is work and professional relationships. Because these are usually based in hierarchical and patriarchal systems, "power over" and the fear of job loss or stagnation are contributing factors. Yet another source is the frustration and stress of daily living: the many stressors of a fast-paced technological and individualistic society, including the competition of getting to the top.

Who or what receives our anger energy? The receivers of our anger are those same persons, circumstances and events that are the stimuli of the anger in the first place. "Self, God, family, friends, partners, our workplace colleagues, unjust situations are some of the many receivers we vent our anger on or toward," affirm Tim La Haye and Bob Phillips in *Anger Is a Choice*.[14]

All aspects of our anger are intricately interwoven. Everyday hurts and frustrations as well as protracted ones contribute to our anger responses.

Two Anger Sequences

From my own experience, I have noted two anger sequence patterns based on the approaches identified above. Each sequence helps interpret the physiological arousal.

In the first sequence, I am in a meeting, giving the much-awaited budget forecast for our salaries. In the midst of my report, someone interrupts me, saying, "Come on, give us the truth and stop fudging the figures." In this situation, I first experience a physiological change in my body. I can feel my face turning red and my heart beginning to pound (biological). Next, I interpret this arousal as a perceived rejection by this person (cognitive). Third, with this interpretation, I decide how I am going to respond (behaviourist). This, of course, brings me back to the conflict transformation repertoire. I may choose, in the interests of this important meeting, to coast, recognizing that the comments came out of that person's concern about salary cuts and had nothing to do with me personally. Or I might carefront (use "I" statements), since this behaviour has effects on other staff members. Alternatively, I could conciliate for now and carefront afterwards. In each instance, I am using the energy of anger in conscious, rational, nonviolent and life-giving ways.

In the second sequence, I am in a crowded elevator when it stops yet again and another passenger gets on. Lost in my own thoughts, I don't look up at who got on last. Then I feel a sharp object on my foot. This is the stimulus. I look up and see that the passenger who just got on the elevator is a blind person with a cane who is trying to find some space. It was the cane I felt on my foot. My interpretation of this stimulus is immediate, and I feel compassion for the blind person rather than annoyance. With this interpretation, the physical response in my body does not put me in a fight or flight preparedness (behaviourist approach). The stimulus occurs (physical approach); then right away, because of that stimulus, I am able to psychologically interpret (cognitive approach) it as nonthreatening (psychodynamic approach) and, consequently, there is limited physiological reaction in my body. Homeostasis prevails.

In each situation, there was a sequence but with a different ebb and flow, both of which were under my conscious control. In other words, with anger as a rational emotion, I author my own anger. Nobody else makes me angry. We are each responsible for our own anger. As a corollary, this means that we are not responsible for anyone else's anger.

The sequences I have just described happen instantaneously, so it is difficult for us to absorb the fact that we both own and author the anger. It comes from our perception of the particular stimulus and its psychological and spiritual effects on us. Because we have gone through similar sequences time and again, they have become part of us. They are now ingrained, and so do not take any amount of time to arrive at, as they did when we were first learning the sequences. For this reason, it may feel like we did not make a decision but, in fact, we did. We decided how to express this anger energy based on responses made in the past. Our responses are learned patterns. These anger sequences are constructs to help us deal nonviolently with our anger energy. They can help us slow down the process of what happens when we experience anger.

20-80 Principle

In many instances of anger arousal, 20 per cent of our reaction is related to the stimulus at hand, and 80 per cent to anger we have suppressed. This blocked chronic anger energy stored in our body, psyche and spirit becomes our anger response to situational anger. I am proposing four styles of anger communication: passive, aggressive, passive-aggressive and assertive. In the rest of this chapter, we explore the first three as further consciousness-raising for assertive nonviolent anger communication, which I cover in Part V.

Anger Communication Styles

> *A relationship will only be as good as its communication.*
>
> David Augsburger

Linear Model of Communication

The linear, sender-receiver model of communication is probably the one most of us are familiar with. Based on the mechanistic worldview of our old story, it postulates one "objective" (correct) reality. A good communicator, using precise and correct words, conveys that reality to the receiver. The receiver must interpret the words in one way: that of the sender. This model precludes any real dialogue.

Circular Model of Communication

The circular model of communication, based on our new story, postulates that communication is constructed as it happens. This is a dynamic process in which the realities of both speaker and listener are co-constructed in a listening-dialogue stance. Meaning and understanding are created and shared by the people involved. Communication is much more complex, interconnected and interdependent than our mechanistic worldview allowed.

Communication is a dynamic process of coordinating the energies of our listening and speaking for union with another, the goal of which is to share and receive meanings related to our observations, thoughts, feelings and needs. For David Augsburger, "A good relationship is two-way communication. To love another is to invite, support, protect that person's equal right to hear and be heard."[15]

Tannen's research[16] suggests that men have been socialized to be more direct and specific in their communication, while women tend to be more indirect and general because of their socialization and sex-role stereotyping. Indirect communication leads to conflict and misunderstandings. Women and men are like two different cultures with two ways of communicating, which makes it difficult for each to understand the another.

Constructive and nonviolent communication, paramount for expressing our conflict and anger, requires balance: directness is needed for clarity, and indirectness is needed for relationship affect. Being direct without being offensive, abusive or causing another to lose face is a skill that can be learned.

Verbal and Nonverbal Components

> *Words are, of course, the most powerful drug used*
> *by [hu]mankind.*
>
> Rudyard Kipling

We communicate with far more than just words. The verbal or linguistic component of communication is the content. It includes choice of words (vocabulary), meaning (semantics), grammar (syntax) and the practicality of the speech (pragmatics). The nonverbal or paralinguistic component of communication is the affect or mood associated with the verbal. It includes body posture, facial expression, eye contact and voice nuances (volume, pitch, rate, timbre).

In the North American culture, the verbal aspect of communication constitutes seven per cent of the message; the nonverbal constitutes 93 per cent, including 38 per cent for the voice and 55 per cent for other body language.[17] Clearly, our nonverbal communication speaks more loudly than words.

Mixed Messages

Good communication involves congruence between the verbal and nonverbal, particularly in situations of conflict and anger. When my words and my body language do not match, a mixed message results. If I say, "I'm not angry!" but my face is flushed, my voice is loud and I am tense, you will know that I *am* angry, despite my words to the contrary. When the message is mixed, people inevitably follow the nonverbal cues, which overshadow the words.

In a culture that places great importance on the verbal, silence is a vacuum that must be filled. Thomas Merton, a Trappist monk, referred to silence as the mother of communication, an integral part of its ebb and flow. Healthy silence (as opposed to the silent treatment of aggressive or passive-aggressive anger communication, which is used to punish or control) is necessary in an increasingly noisy world.

Four Communication Styles

Listed here are four of the most common communication styles. Note that the fourth – assertive – is the only healthy one on the list and, it is hoped, the one we use most. But, amidst the stress and tension of conflict and anger, we may also use the other three at times.

TABLE — ANGER COMMUNICATION STYLES

1. **passive** (Latin *patior*: endure, suffer): I suffer.
2. **aggressive** (Latin *aggredi*: move forward/against): You suffer.
3. **passive-aggressive** (*patior* + *aggredi*): We both suffer.
4. **assertive** (Latin *ad* + *sere*: to join): We both learn and grow.

Unhealthy Anger Communication

When angry, count to four. When very angry, swear.

Mark Twain

Passive, aggressive and passive-aggressive communication styles comprise varying degrees of violent, unconstructive and even destructive ways of communicating. Each is related to our level of self-knowledge, self-acceptance and self-esteem, and reflects our emotional state in a given encounter. Becoming aware of which style(s) we use, and when, can help us move forward on the journey to a life of nonviolence.

Let's take a closer look at the three unhealthy anger communication styles.

Passive Anger Communication

What does passive anger communication look like and sound like? When we express our anger passively, we are concerned about being liked and accepted; we fear rejection. We may feel powerless, controlled, victimized. Driven by our fear of rejection, we sound tentative because we want to please at all costs.

A cluster of characteristics, including self-blaming, self-sacrificing, dispassionate, ineffectual, manipulative communication, may be indicative of this style.[18] When safety issues surface, we may use this style because we have no self-empowering alternative.

Passive communication ends with an upward questioning inflection or questions such as "Isn't that right?" or "Can't you see?" or "I'm not sure?" Nonverbally, we may have limited eye contact, slumping body posture, nervous tics and a monotonous voice. We may mumble, cover our mouth or whisper when speaking. When asked to repeat what we've said, but more loudly, we pull back with, "Oh, it's nothing…." As Robert Bolton, author of *People Skills*, explains, "Many submissive (passive) people do not express their honest feelings, needs, values, and concerns. They allow others to violate their space, deny their rights, and ignore their needs. These people rarely state their desires...or do so in an apologetic and diffident manner."[19]

Physical Manifestations

Our unhealthy expressions of anger can be both covert and overt. When we express anger indirectly, it is covert, passive and internalized anger; it affects us more than the other person. With no outward signs of our true feelings, the anger might seem cold and unthinking.

Covert, passive anger can be related to physical ailments. While we may be genetically predisposed to certain health problems (such as strokes, diabetes or cancer), stress from bottled-up anger can exacerbate existing conditions or pave the way for other stress-linked illnesses. Other ways of somatizing our anger include the misuse or abuse of food (overeating, undereating), alcohol and drugs.

Psychological Manifestations

Covert, passive anger is also internalized psychologically, and is linked to such problems as boredom, depression and passive-aggressiveness. When I experience anger but do not express it, this unprocessed, stored energy slips out in subtle ways. I feel bored, neglected and unloved.

Spiritual Manifestations

Internalized anger energy can also be exhibited through spiritual ennui, a general lack of groundedness and unfocused goals and values. A spirituality of nonviolence as a way of life makes us more aware, helping us recognize passive anger communication.

Aggressive Anger Communication

An aggressive anger communication style is loud, with cursing, swearing and other types of verbal obscenities. A lot of blaming "you" statements are used: "You make me so angry" or "It's all your fault" or "You are such a loser; I wish I had never met you." Confrontational and offensive, the aggressive style focuses on getting our needs met at others' expense.

Aggressive anger is directed outward toward the one with whom I'm angry. Like overt anger, it has a number of violent manifestations: power over, threatening, bullying, unjust blaming, revenge and character assassination. When we are aggressive we tend to be hostile, domineering, antagonistic, know-it-all and self-righteous. Aggressive anger, says David Johnson in his book *Reaching Out*, "is an attempt to hurt someone or destroy someone. It infringes on the rights of others and involves expressing my feelings through insults, sarcasm, put downs and hostile statements and actions…. It violates others' rights to be treated with respect and dignity."[20]

This destructive and unhealthy expression of anger is manifested by physical and psychological hostility, including displaced hostility (anger redirected onto someone or something less threatening). For example, when I am upset with my boss but do not deal with the conflict and anger because of the possible personal repercussions, I may express it in road rage on the way home, displacing my anger on an innocent motorist because of some minor slip-up (the 20-80 principle). Or I may turn the anger on someone at home who is lower down on the "power over" scale.

Physical Manifestations

The physical manifestations of aggressive anger expression can include shouting, pointing and jabbing, which can quickly move to pushing, shoving, hitting, slapping, and even maiming and killing. This type of violent behaviour, endemic in our society, is anger expression out of control.

Psychological Manifestations

Psychological manifestations of aggressive anger display are harder to spot because there is no physical harm, no bruises, no broken bones on the person receiving this anger – only sarcasm, belittling, gossip, lies and even character assassination. However, this anger is unmistakable. When we express our anger aggressively, we overpower and dominate others; the psychological scars on the person receiving this negative energy are incalculable. This style can also take the form of blaming the other for our anger.

Passive-Aggressive Anger Communication

Communication particular to passive-aggressive anger is not noticeably different from the tentative, reticent and fawning style of passive anger communication. Over the years, the one difference I have noted is that there are more surface niceties with the "yes, yes" stance, and, at the same time, more "leaking" of the suppressed anger through mismatched verbal and nonverbal aspects.

This destructive anger expression is a combination of both the passive and the aggressive anger communication styles. Because I may be concerned about my reputation, my job or my persona, I cannot act out my frustration or hurt in aggressive ways. Instead, I do this passive-aggressively in subtle and insidious ways.

A passive-aggressive anger communication style causes violence to both parties in the conflict. Its goal is revenge. It is the most common form of anger expression in hierarchical, patriarchal closed systems in which power over and subtle threats of failing, firing, limited advancement and rejection result in overt dependence and submissiveness. It is probably the most difficult expression of anger to deal with, because it is integral to the norms and taboos of a system that distrusts and discourages conflict and anger. Ironically, in such dualistic systems with a purported zero tolerance for violence, passive-aggressive energy is rampant.

Physical and Psychological Manifestations

It is important to note that this type of anger expression is often unconscious. Because I do not allow myself to get angry, I repress it but it leaks out. On the surface, the passive-aggressive anger style looks very much like the passive anger style. It is externally reticent, tentative, docile, nice and accommodating. On closer observation, some definite manifestations of aggression exist. When we are passive-aggressive, we keep a mental tally of perceived hurts and injustices and eventually take our revenge.

Its most common manifestations include physical and emotional distancing and the silent treatment (refusing to speak to the other person as punishment).[21] A variation on this silent treatment is sending a memo or an e-mail to someone when a face-to-face encounter is both possible and necessary. Not returning phone calls or e-mail messages can be other examples of passive-aggressive behaviour.

A passive-aggressive anger style can also include breaking promises and then denying I had made such a promise, or agreeing to a particular decision or a plan of action and then covertly sabotaging it.

Yet another manifestation is double-booking meetings and appointments, or arriving late and leaving early: saying "yes" but acting "no." When I do this, I cause disruptions and then I complain about not hearing about certain things that are going on, things I have missed because of these passive-aggressive behaviours.

Other behaviours are generalized whining and complaining – not directly to the persons concerned but in their presence, hoping they "catch on," or triangulation. I speak to "C" about the issues I have with "B" in the hopes that it will get back to "B" and she or he will shape up.

Spiritual Manifestations

The spiritual manifestations of this type of anger expression are also subtle, because of the lack of congruence in our life. On the one hand, we purport to be spiritual and yet, on the other, our passive, aggressive and passive-aggressive anger expressions eat away at any ongoing sense of spiritual transformation. We may loudly decry such behaviours in others and be self-righteous in condoning our own violent behaviours. At times, there may be such a disconnect within us that we cannot even name this contradiction. For example, I have noted in some groups of people who live consecrated lives that there is both a deep desire for holiness and strong norms and taboos about conflict and anger. Violence can result in many of these communal situations, most often in passive-aggressiveness.

Anger is necessary for us to grow into wholeness and holiness. At the same time, we need to be aware of, and temper, our anger energy.

Why Do We Get Angry?

Anger results from something being amiss: we feel a sense of diminishment, frustration or injustice. However, we can also become angry as a way to control situations and other people. With *instrumental anger*, we lash out until we get our way, like a toddler having a temper tantrum.

Cathartic anger stems from a build-up of tension or stress: when we can't contain it, we have to release it.

Anyone who is *chronically angry* tends to be cynical, bitter and negative. Anger is directed outward, and is destructive to all parties. When we are chronically angry, we have great difficulty letting go: of the specific hurt at hand, but also of our victim identity. We reach a point at which we lose the essence of who we are apart from being a victim. To let go of this acquired identity is scary because, without it, we would no longer know who we are.

We must know ourselves well enough to understand when we use anger manipulatively and selfishly (instrumental), when it is lack of control (cathartic), and when it is a harbouring of hurts and grudges that have never been dealt with and released (chronic anger and victim identity).

The assertive anger communication style is the goal for each of us in transforming our anger energy, with listening-dialogue and communion the expression of this style. I have developed an anger communication survey, "Anger Response Styles: A Self-Assessment" (Appendix A, with directions for completion and scoring). Quick and easy to use, this self-assessment can help with the consciousness-raising needed for healthy anger communication.

PART IV: REFLECTION AND DISCUSSION STARTERS

1. Do you agree that anger is a secondary emotion? Explain.

2. Emotions involve judgment and choice and are rational. Discuss.

3. Are you ambivalent towards your anger? What is your favourite euphemism to indicate you are angry?

4. Anger is socially constructed. Cultures deal with its energy differently. Discuss.

5. How do women and men deal with their anger as determined by their gender socialization?

6. Discuss the American Psychological Association's statement that we are not genetically disposed to violence.

7. Explore the nature/nurture debate regarding personality and anger.

8. What is your definition of intrapersonal anger? Interpersonal anger? Which approach(es) helps you understand your anger: biological, psychoanalytical, behaviourist, cognitive?

9. What happens in your body when you become angry? Which anger sequence helps you understand your anger energy?

10. Name the most common causes of your anger. Who are the people most often involved in your anger?

11. Discuss the linear and circular models of communication. Which one do you use?

12. Reflect on the physical, psychological and spiritual manifestations of passive, aggressive and passive-aggressive anger communication styles.

PART V

NONVIOLENT ANGER COMMUNICATION

10

ANGER ENERGY: PHYSICAL AND PSYCHOLOGICAL TRANSFORMATION

Anger channelled appropriately can help us solve our problems.

Jan Stratton

5 A's

In Part V, we learn how to communicate our anger in assertive, healthy and non-violent ways, flowing from a spirituality of nonviolence and quantum principles of interdependence, reciprocity, mutuality and equality.

Do you ever express gratitude for anger as a gift in your life? I have designed the 5 A's of Anger Transformation – awareness, acceptance, analysis, appropriate action and appreciation – to help us recognize the gift of our anger.[1] Once we learn the process, following it becomes automatic, even in the "heat of the moment."

TABLE — 5 A's OF ANGER TRANSFORMATION

1. Awareness
2. Acceptance
3. Analysis
4. Appropriate Action
5. Appreciation

The process is not so much linear as an immediate awareness of what is happening within and without. Its constructs can help us move from violence to nonviolence, from destructive to constructive anger expression.

1. Awareness

Because we deny anger in our lives, we have many ways to bury it deep within and many passive, aggressive and passive-aggressive styles of handling it. Awareness is learning to recognize the signs of anger energy in our body, psyche and spirit. It is knowing who we are, naming and accepting our anger as a God-given energy for protection and growth.

In the anger management workshops I facilitate, many participants are not aware of how they carry anger in their bodies; they may even deny something is amiss.

Our dualistic training has made many of us uncomfortable with, and in, our bodies. We may live as though only the spiritual counts, with the material body being inferior and less important. As a result, we may see our bodies as objects and adhere to society's norms about how we should look, what we should weigh, and how we should dress. This is particularly (but not exclusively) the case for women.

To see our bodies as "subjects" and as "temples of God" means learning to be more comfortable with and aware of our bodies as integral to who we are. In this way we can become aware of the physical changes that occur when we are angry. A flushed face, a pounding heart, faintness or cold hands may be signals that something is wrong.

With awareness of bodily changes, we become aware of psychological and spiritual changes. When we feel hurt, frustrated, diminished, put down, rejected or betrayed, our psyche and spirit tell us this through our anger.

2. Acceptance

Being aware of the anger energy and the resulting changes in my body, mind and spirit, I can move to accept it and take personal responsibility for it. I am the author of my own anger, despite any extenuating circumstances. Psychologically and spiritually, I acknowledge that, indeed, I am angry because of what has happened. My feelings of hurt, frustration and diminishment may be hidden beneath the anger, but they are there, waiting to be explored. When I accept that I am angry based on my perceptions and then accept this anger with gentleness, I can move forward. I regain personal control as I accept anger in my life. What I choose to do with this energy moves me to analyze or evaluate the situation.

3. Analysis

Here I determine what to do with my anger energy. I might look at the anger sequences noted above to determine how serious or threatening the situation is to me. I recognize that anger is simply a distress signal. I look at the who, what and why of this anger. Is it a minor frustration that I must express and let go of? Is the anger part of a serious conflict that must be dealt with to release the energy?

In this analysis I look at both the intrapersonal and interpersonal aspects of the situation. Is my perception of the hurt part of the other person's baggage and incompleteness, or was it intended? What are the effects of the hurt on me? My analysis of these factors determines whether I am going to get angry, how intense the anger will be, and for how long I will stay angry. This aspect of the process takes only seconds with our body, mind and psyche on alert.

4. Appropriate Action

In this step, which follows quickly from analysis, I make a conscious choice about how to enact this anger energy. "There are risks in expressing it; there are risks in not expressing it," explains David W. Johnson in *Reaching Out: Interpersonal Effectiveness and Self-Actualization*.[2] I can choose to follow up on the particular situation (carefrontation, concession, conciliation, cooperation); I can delay it; or I can decide I am not going to deal with it overtly because it is not safe, or it is not important enough (coasting). No matter what my decision is, I make it consciously, constructively and nonviolently, using assertive communication and listening-dialogue.

5. Appreciation

Once I have gone through the first four parts of this process, which takes very little time in most situations, I appreciate this self-growth and self-integration in a reflective moment.

Constructive, Healthy, Nonviolent Anger

> *Anyone can become angry – that is easy.*
> *But to be angry with the right person,*
> *to the right degree, at the right time,*
> *for the right purpose and in the right way –*
> *this is not easy.*

Aristotle

Aristotle is suggesting, in the above epigraph, that balance is the key to expressing our frustration, anger and rage nonviolently. This involves accepting the energies of these emotions and expressing them in healthy ways. David Augsburger points out in *Caring Enough to Confront*, "The energies of anger can flow in self-affirming ways when directed by love – the awareness of the other person's equal preciousness. Anger energies become a creative force when they are employed to change my own behaviour... and to confront the other with his or her need to change unloving behaviour. Anger is a positive emotion, a self-affirming emotion which responds reflexively to the threat of rejection or devaluation."[3]

The Five A's of anger transformation set the stage for specific how to's in assertive, constructive, nonviolent anger. The mnemonic ANGER can help focus this discussion.

TABLE — ANGER MNEMONIC

A: assertive, articulate

N: nonviolent, never-ending

G: God-given, goal-directed

E: essential, energizing

R: responsible, respectful

Assertive Anger Communication Style

A kind word is like a spring day.

Russian Proverb

Physical Manifestations

In Part IV, we looked at the four anger communication styles we use, focusing on the first three, which are unhealthy and violent. Now we will explore the fourth: healthy, assertive, constructive and nonviolent anger expression, both for the one who is angry and the one who is on the receiving end of that anger. It is a both/and style that takes care of my needs, my rights, and at the same time, respects yours.

Assertive anger communication involves less stress than the other types of anger expression. Given that it takes courage to become self-empowered and risk when I share something difficult with another, the type of stress tends to be more eustress than the distress of the other three styles. Hence, my body, psyche and spirit feel less tension, which is obvious in my nonverbal body language, including facial expression, eye contact, and volume and tone of voice.

Psychological and Spiritual Manifestations

The psychological and spiritual manifestations of assertive anger communication are in line with its nonverbal manifestations. From a spirituality of nonviolence, speaking the truth in love means praying about the relationship and how to say what needs to be said. At the same time, in the ebb and flow of listening-dialogue, I stay grounded in Jesus' assurance, "Do not become anxious about how or what you should speak ... for the Holy Spirit will teach you in that very hour what you ought to say" (Luke 12:11-12). How do we let go of this anxiety? We have to learn how.

Personal "I" Statements

The hallmark of an assertive anger communication style is ownership of the anger and feelings of hurt, frustration and diminishment. In my communication with you about the situation, I use "I" statements. No matter what the circumstances of the conflict are, I do not blame you, judge you or evaluate you for what I am feeling. "Healthy self-assertiveness is not hostile, abusive, or sarcastic," says Nathaniel Branden.[4] Rather, my communication is overt, direct, honest and shared from my personal perceptions. Assertive behaviour means revealing your feelings, thoughts, opinions and preferences to the other person in an honest and appropriate way that respects both parties.

Such ownership statements have evolved from programs such as Thomas Gordon's Parent Effectiveness Training programs (PET) and Teacher Effectiveness Training programs (TET). Originally called "I messages," with three parts, today they are usually called "I" statements, with four parts.

TABLE — PERSONAL "I" STATEMENTS

1. I feel... [Name the emotion.]
2. When you... [State the other's concrete action.]
3. Because... [State the effect on you.]
4. I would appreciate... [Share what would help you next time.]

Because a trust relationship already exists, the personal "I" statement is an invitation to both listening and dialogue. Your listening to my sharing my vulnerability, and my owning my anger in this situation, invite you to own the problem with me. Together, we can look at possible ways of dealing with it together. Then the process is reversed. I listen to your feelings and remain open to your sharing this problem as ours.

An example of a personal "I" statement follows.

TABLE — EXAMPLE: PERSONAL "I" STATEMENT

1. **I feel... [Name the emotion.]** "I feel angry [or annoyed, or frustrated, or] ...

2. **When you... [State the other's concrete action.]** "When you didn't put gas in the car last night after you used it."

3. **Because... [State the effect on you.]** "Because I had to find a gas station early this morning and as a result, I was late for my 7:30 meeting."

4. **I would appreciate... [Share what would help you next time.]** "I would appreciate it if, next Wednesday, before you bring the car home, you ensure it has enough gas, since I have a 7:30 a.m. meeting on Thursday."

A key point to remember is that when I suggest to the other what I would appreciate or what I need, it is just that: a suggestion. The other may not agree to it. Rather, adult to adult, I am stating my needs assertively, recognizing that these may or may not be taken care of. In stating them, I have empowered myself and have done all I can.

Professional "I" Statements

When I began facilitating communication workshops, I used the "I" statement format for all situations. One group of high school principals, many of whom were men, literally refused even to try "I" statements in role-play situations.

Clearly, using such statements could make people in positions of power too vulnerable in their professional lives. Such shared feelings could be used against them in a hierarchical organization. As I reflected on their resistance, I realized that if professionals were going to use these statements, they would have to be adapted. From this difficult experience, I developed what I call professional "I" statements, which are different from personal ones. In professional "I" statements, I omitted the "feelings" aspect and added observations (not judgments or evaluations).

TABLE — PROFESSIONAL "I" STATEMENTS

1. I observed, saw, noted, learned... [Cite the specific, concrete observation.]
2. I think, I know... [State your ideas and thoughts on the topic in ways that are nonjudgmental and nonevaluative.]
3. I would appreciate/like... OR, I need... [State your concrete need/wish.]

Take the example of two employees who apply for a promotion. Both are qualified, but each has different strengths. How can the one who does not get the promotion communicate her or his anger, hurt and disappointment? How does this person become self-empowered? The following professional "I" statement offers an example of assertive, direct and nonviolent communication.

TABLE — EXAMPLE: PROFESSIONAL "I" STATEMENT

1. **I noticed... I learned... [Cite the specific, concrete observation.]** "I learned that another employee got the promotion I applied for."

2. **I think... I know... [State your ideas and thoughts on the topic in ways that are nonjudgmental and nonevaluative.]** "I know I am qualified for the job. You stated in my interview that I had solid training and experience."

3. **I would appreciate... [State your concrete need/wish.]** "To help me learn from this interview, I would appreciate knowing why I did not get the promotion."

We have looked at the physical, psychological and spiritual manifestations of assertive anger communication, including the components of both personal and professional "I" statements. While they are not quick fixes, these statements offer us concrete ways to express our anger assertively and nonviolently, based on the principles of mutuality and reciprocity. A number of names for assertive anger communication – including constructive, nonviolent, purposeful, healthy, creative, effective and situational – connote accepting this energy as an invaluable means of growth and change. A more recent and popular name is Marshall Rosenberg's *nonviolent communication* (NVC). Its principles are based on simplicity, patience and compassion with oneself and others, doing what we already know but have been taught to forget. Its four components, which are almost identical to "I" statements, focus our attention on the observations, feelings, needs and requests of both parties.

Anger Energy: Physical Transformation

Releasing Anger Energy Nonviolently

In Chapter 5 we looked at *eustress* and *distress*, exploring the physiological changes for each. Anger is a signal of distress.

An obvious question is what to do with the fight-flight build-up of adrenaline and noradrenaline in our bodies when learning how to handle our anger in healthy ways. A constant state of equilibrium would lead to stagnation, while a constant state of high alert would be hard on our bodies. How do we achieve a balance?

Various therapies offer ways of dealing with anger, seeing the need to drain the excess build-up in the body. The challenge is to do so nonviolently, as violence begets violence. Some therapists use cathartic techniques: pounding, hitting, punching, venting or screaming.[5] But when I vent, pound and punch, I once again put my body in a state of alert, with adrenaline and noradrenaline being pumped into the bloodstream. Physiological testing has shown the energy is not released; the body does not reach any homeostasis and the cause of the anger is not let go psychologically and spiritually.

Walking, running, jogging, swimming, aerobics, yoga, aquacise and cycling are helpful ways to release the energy of anger. Others include pottery, woodworking, painting, sewing or knitting; cleaning, baking, doing laundry, mowing the lawn or gardening; listening to music, reading and writing poetry, reading books, doing crosswords and jigsaw puzzles. Some people enjoy sitting and rocking, since the rhythmic movement soothes their jangled body. Others work with trained professionals who help them release the pent-up energy.

Anger Energy: Psychological Transformation

Our Experiences of Anger: After, Before, During

How can we use our thoughts, as well as our bodies and spirits, to help transform our anger energy?

Post mortems – literally, "after deaths" – are a way to examine things once the damage is done. When I began to recognize that I was doing post mortems of experiences in my own life, I saw how they could be used to help with the psychological transformation of my anger in nonviolent yet practical ways. Over time, I developed an "after, before and during" sequence based on the cognitive repatterning approach to anger, noted above. The three create a whole: what to do "after the fact"; how to prepare "before the fact"; and what to do "during the fact." These approaches happen simultaneously, since conflict and anger are ever present in our lives. We might be dealing with one situation that has just happened, preparing for another and in the midst of still another.

Recall the anger sequence based on the cognitive approach: I experience a stimulus in my body and, aware of it, I interpret it, which leads me to specify the emotion I am experiencing. It would be wonderful if we could do this as the anger stimulus occurs, but most of us become aware only after the fact. Until we become aware of and accept our anger energy situationally, awareness after the fact seems the place to start. In these post mortems, we cognitively repattern our anger reaction.

TABLE — PSYCHOLOGICAL ANGER TRANSFORMATION

After: Replay, Redo, Repattern

Before: Rehearse

During: Respect

After the Fact: How to Replay, Redo, Repattern

No doubt you have caught yourself doing "after the fact" post mortems of what you should have said and done in a conflict and anger situation, usually from a vengeance perspective: "I should have said…, and that would have taken the wind out of her/his sails!" "I should have done…, and that would have shown her/him who's boss!"

Post mortems can be negative if they function simply to solidify our resentment, cynicism, despair, or desire for retaliation or revenge or to deepen a pervasive unhappiness with ourselves and others. Learning how to use them in a constructive way can help foster our nonviolence.

First, I *replay* the situation in a quiet, even prayerful, context. This can help me get a better perspective in a stress-free and relaxing environment. Visualizing, I replay the situation just as it happened, with particular attention to what I said and did.

Next, I *redo* or rescript my part, drawing on my grounded, assertive and non-violent self to choose the words and actions. How do I wish I had responded to what the other said and did? My choice of words and actions must be both self-empowering and respectful.

Finally, I *repattern* my thoughts so I am ready to handle a similar situation in the future. No two situations are ever the same, but our anger responses may be much the same from years of practice. Cognitive repatterning helps us learn how to change our anger responses because we cannot change the other person. Here are two exercises that can help us become more aware of the other as a person and not just as our enemy.

The *empty chair exercise* is a variation of repatterning we can do in private or with the help of a trusted friend or counsellor. Taking two chairs, I sit in one and face the empty one, and replay the whole situation, first saying what I would have liked to have said and done in nonviolent ways. Then I move across to the empty chair and I respond. I say what I think the other person would like to have said and done. This is a wonderful way to truly listen to and respect the best in the other person, and can soften my own heart towards her or him.

Another cognitive repatterning exercise is *writing a letter* to the other person to express anger and hurt in constructive, nonjudgmental and non-blaming ways. The letter is never sent; rather, it is an opportunity to get in touch with what is below the surface of our anger. We can also respond to the letter from the other person's perspective to become aware of his or her journey to growth and trans-formation. Some people suggest a ritual burning of the letter, symbolizing the release of new-found energy into the universe. Variations on the letter-writing exercise are journalling and poetry writing, which can also help in using our post mortems positively and constructively.

Before the Fact: How to Rehearse

Psychological management of anger can also happen before the fact; I call this *rehearsal*. This exercise is more straightforward because we all tend to prepare for important events. When I know in advance that there will be a certain meeting or situation in which there could be conflict and intense emotions, including anger, I rehearse what I would like to say and do.

In a quiet and prayerful atmosphere, I visualize how the stressful scenario might unfold. "If so and so says…, I will respond with…." Obviously, the way I envisage the event is my perception of the energies involved. I rehearse how I want to respond in the worst-case and best-case scenarios. As with life, the actual scenario will be neither of these rehearsed scenarios; the goal of this cognitive rehearsal is to prepare my heart to be open to my own energy and needs as well as those of the other person. It prepares me to respond constructively and nonviolently, no matter how the situation plays out.

The aim of rehearsal is to change my heart of stone (right/wrong, win/lose) to a nonviolent heart of flesh (Ezekiel 36:26). It keeps me open to those whisperings of listening-dialogue that are so essential to our growth. As we prepare, we can change our counterproductive mindsets, free ourselves from entrenched positions, and increase our openness to meeting mutual needs and interests and engaging in creative problem solving.

During the Fact: How to Respect

After-the-fact and before-the-fact strategies are designed to help us deal with an actual anger situation during the fact.

One aspect of psychological anger transformation is the listening-dialogue approach we explored above. Integral to the dialogue aspect are "I" statements. In the listening aspect, I let the other person speak without interruption, correction, retaliation or blaming. As Harriet Goldhor Lerner states in *The Dance of Connection*, "When we listen to another person with attention and care, we validate and deepen the connection between us."[6]

The underlying premise in listening-dialogue is that each has a turn to share and a turn to listen. This is where self-talk is important. Self-talk is that internal monologue that keeps us grounded and respectful when listening:

* "Okay, breathe deeply; you will have your turn to share your story."

* "So, that is how she/he interprets what I said/did."

* "Keep quiet and listen; you don't know all the facts."

I listen out of my wisdom, a wisdom that knows when to speak and when to keep its own counsel, a wisdom that flows from a spirituality of nonviolence. For Ann Sutton, author of *Thriving on Stress*, "Good listening is the key to skillful communication. It is one of the most priceless gifts we can offer other people. When a person feels listened to, they feel accepted, valued, respected, heard and understood."[7]

The 5 A's in Practice

In the instantaneous flash of awareness, acceptance and analysis of my anger in a situation, I know the appropriate action I need to take with this person, in this context and at this time. As I live out of a spirituality of nonviolence, I intuit from the ebb and flow of the situation what to do.

11

ANGER ENERGY: SPIRITUAL TRANSFORMATION

When someone forgives a person,... it is the forgiver who changes.

Michael E. McCullough

Forgiveness

Forgiveness and reconciliation are the two processes in the spiritual transformation of our anger energy. Though sometimes used synonymously, they are not identical. Forgiveness is about self-healing; reconciliation is mutual healing, mutual forgiveness.

I see forgiveness as a deeply spiritual process, interdependently related to anger and the transformation of its energy. In my initial work in this field in the 1980s, I could find very little in the literature on forgiveness, particularly its spiritual aspects. This gap set me on the path of doing research and writing on forgiveness, and facilitating forgiveness workshops and retreats. Researchers did not begin to explore the concept of forgiveness as integral to anger until the last 20 years of the 20th century, and then it was studied as a psychosocial construct and a human value.[1] That is beginning to change.

What Is Forgiveness?

> The stupid either forgive or forget
> The naive forgive and forget
> The wise forgive but do not forget.

Thomas Szasz

Many of us were taught to "forgive and forget." I suggest we learn to forgive and remember – not in a vindictive way, but in a healthy way. This approach helps us move away from our resentment and the desire for revenge. Forgiveness is all about self-healing. When I "re-member" something or someone, I connect aspects of myself that have been cut off.

We can handle the intense energy of some conflict/anger situations as they happen, forgiving and reconciling almost immediately. Other instances involve intense turmoil and suffering that we will never forget. These are called critical incidents (traumas) because they touch the core of who we are and change our lives irrevocably. Things may never be the same after a critical incident, but we can, and must, move on so we can lead healthier physical, psychological and spiritual lives. During this holistic process of forgiveness, we use our inner resources, the help of friends, a therapist and God to be healed and let go of our desire for punishment and revenge. As Kathleen Fischer suggests in *Moving On*, "In the process of remembering, we create a new story...a fresh pattern of meaning emerges."[2] We forgive.

As I let go of my desire to get even with or punish the other person, I choose not to use this situation against this person in future and not to gossip about it. I also stop punishing myself by releasing the energy I have been using to keep the hurt alive. When the hurt surfaces within me, I refuse to ruminate on it, keep it alive or become a victim. I show forbearance and compassion. "Holding onto the pain, embarrassment, or anger, continually causes you to revisit the past and infects the present," explains Gillian Stokes in *Forgiveness: Wisdom from Around the World*. "The event that caused you pain is over though its consequences may remain with you for the rest of your life. The sooner you release your attachment to your negative memories, the sooner you can recover and rebuild your life."[3]

For this healing to happen, we must understand the various types of forgiveness. Forgiveness is a way of life based on a spirituality of nonviolence and a recognition of our interconnectedness; it is also an attitude, a decision and a process. Forgiveness is holistic; it affects all areas of our lives. Our anger transformation is physical, psychological and spiritual.

Types of Forgiveness

> *To err is human, to forgive divine.*
>
> Alexander Pope

Because forgiveness is ongoing and lifelong, because I may not want to forgive in the beginning, because of my guilt and perhaps my unconscious holding on to my victim identity, I may go through various types of forgiveness on the journey to wholeness. It is as if I have to work through all the conditions I put on my forgiveness one by one, as I let go of my desire for control and getting even. No wonder, forgiveness is not just a once and for all decision. I may have to forgive a person over and over for the same hurt, because forgiveness takes time.

In the early stages of the process, I gradually move away from *conditional forgiveness*, which says, "I will forgive if…." I begin to recognize that the only person I can change is myself. I let go of my desire to want to control and change you.

Pseudo forgiveness is probably alive and well for many of us. How often have we said the words of forgiveness in perfunctory and unfocused ways, as part of the niceties of life, ("Please forgive me." "I'm sorry!") or as part of our prayer ("Forgive us… as we forgive others…"). *Real forgiveness* demands that we recognize and set aside our ego needs of revenge and retaliation. It focuses on my personal healing and re-membering, not getting even with you.

Forgiveness has to be both from the head and from the heart, a decision and a desire. The decision to forgive is a start, but more is needed. Only when our hearts are full of compassion can we move towards true forgiveness.

To be able to forgive another unconditionally is as close to divine as any of us may get. Yet this is the forgiveness Jesus exemplified and calls us to provide. Knowing that God loves and forgives us can help us to do the same for others.

The Process of Forgiveness

The following four-step process can help us learn how to become forgiving people.

TABLE — PROCESS OF FORGIVENESS

1. Naming
2. Owning
3. Blessing
4. Letting go and moving on

Step 1: Naming

When I can name my hurt and pain, I have embarked on the first step of the process of forgiveness. I begin to move away from denying or suppressing the anger/conflict, from downplaying it, and rationalizing that it was not as bad as I remember it. I also move away from self-blame and let go of the secrecy, shame and guilt associated with the incident. By telling my story of hurt to a trusted listener, such as a friend or counsellor, or by writing it in a journal, I give it a voice that has otherwise been heard only inside my body, psyche and spirit. As I tell my story in words, remembering the details of what another said or did and how this affected me, I feel believed and accepted.

The offending person may never know I was hurt. Because forgiveness is a personal decision and process, I do not need the other person's knowledge, permission or approval to forgive her or him. Forgiveness can also happen even if that person is dead. With grace, I alone make the decision to forgive.

Step 2: Owning

When I own the hurt related to my anger, I allow myself to feel fully in the depths of my body, spirit and psyche the pain I have denied, buried or rationalized. Part of this step involves expressing in my body the depth of my anguish, because my body has a memory, and the energy holding this hurt may be blocked in my body. Owning releases that blocked body energy. (Some people may need to work with a trained professional for this step.)

Owning acknowledges that my emotions are normal and natural and that I am the author of my anger; no one else can make me feel an emotion. I move away from blaming ("You hurt me; you made me so angry") to self-responsibility ("I felt angry and hurt when you…").

Many people get stuck at this stage of forgiveness because subconsciously or unconsciously they find a certain security in being a victim. Blaming and learned helplessness become a way of life. When we hold on to a hurt or a grudge for years and years, a part of us dies: our self-esteem, our spontaneity, our laughter, our energy, our dreams. We remain victims when we relinquish our personal power.

Owning does not mean condoning what has happened. It is not intended to encourage self-blame. Rather, it helps us move away from feeling like a victim. Owning our anger and rage, even in the wake of extreme violence or hurt, frees us from the power of the oppressor.

Step 3: Blessing

Blessing leads to integration. After naming my hurt, and owning it in all its pain, blessing is a gradual move to integrate this experience. I come to see that I am who I am today, because of – not in spite of – that critical incident, that event with all its hurt and pain. Blessing my hurt, my anger, my pain is part of coming home to the whole of me, both my sorrows and my joys, in an acceptance of the ebb and flow of life.

Blessing is all about realizing that, at times, life is not fair, but I can choose what I will do with the injustices I face. If I believe I am interconnected to myself, to others, to God and to the Earth, I integrate who I am and who I am becoming in light of this blessing.

Blessing allows me to live as fully as I can in both the expected and unexpected events of life.

Step 4: Letting Go and Moving On

Maria Harris reminds us in *Proclaim Jubilee*, "Sometimes forgiveness – and the acknowledgement of wrong – takes a long time."[4] Letting go is risky. I may be afraid of getting hurt again, and may even hold on to my hurt because it is "comfortable." But by letting go, we transform anger energy and embrace life again.

Moving on is also risky, but it is necessary if we want to be healthy in body, mind and spirit. I know I am moving on when I have released the energy to focus on the here and now. I no longer need to talk about the incident all the time; I no longer harbour feelings of hate or revenge for the other person; I am able to recall the incident without feeling the horrific hurt and pain that were once integral to it. Although I will always remember the incident with a certain sadness, my physical, psychological and spiritual energies are not totally drained by it.

Moving on does not necessarily mean continuing in or renewing our relationship with the other person. Doing so is not realistic or even safe in some situations. As we integrate what has happened, we may have to end a particular relationship. Or the relationship may continue at a different level.

Forgiveness and Healing Practices

What are some ways we can work through the process of forgiveness and healing? Deep within the intuitive part of our beings, we already know what can help; to these I would add engaging in any nonviolent ritual that both empowers us and respects the other person.

These might include sharing our stories with a trusted friend or counsellor; physically releasing the pent-up energy in our bodies; and the empty-chair process, letter writing, journalling, writing poetry, or music.

Prayer is central to forgiveness; God can be part of any forgiveness we give or receive. The prayer may at first include our anger towards God for what happened and lead into contemplation of the loving mystery of God. It is through our deepening relationship with God that forgiveness as gift and as grace comes, imperceptibly but surely.

Forgiveness: A Way of Life

> *Forgiveness is the fragrance the violet sheds on the heel that has crushed it.*
>
> Mark Twain

Living the Now

Forgiveness as *a way of life* underscores that it is not just a quick fix to re-establish harmony. Rather, as a key part of a spirituality of nonviolence, forgiveness is living one day at a time. It is in the here and now, with respect and regard for all – especially the persons, circumstances and events of today – that I find my forgiving heart of flesh, rather than my heart of stone.

Forgiveness is ultimately *God's grace* with my good intentions and actions, *a gift* that comes to its fullness gradually. "Though we can open ourselves to it and prepare for it, forgiveness of any kind finally comes as a grace," confirms Kathleen Fischer.[5]

Forgiveness is *an attitude*, inviting us to let go of any desire for retaliation and revenge on the one involved in our hurt, anger and diminishment. Feelings of revenge keep us victims; gentleness, on the other hand, recognizes our similarity to our enemy, which can help us respect and value the other for who she or he is, not what she or he has done. Understanding softens our hearts and reminds us that we, too, have hurt others and needed forgiveness.

Forgiveness is *a decision*. We can choose whether we want to get better, releasing the anger energy we have trapped in resentment, or whether we want to remain bitter, with the desire to even the score.

Forgiveness is *ongoing*.

Jesus' Third Way: Love of Enemy

> *A love that is without anger is as worthless as*
> *anger that is without love.*
>
> David Augsburger

Jesus' Anger

Earlier in these pages, I spoke of Jesus' Third Way as a model for dealing with our conflict and anger. Neither passive (flight) nor aggressive (fight), it is based on an assertive and constructive spirituality of nonviolence. Remember Ephesians 4:26: "Be angry but sin not." These words are both an invitation and a challenge to use our God-given emotion of anger, but with awareness and reverence.

Jesus showed us the dynamic tension between being angry and being aware. In Jesus' anger at the moneychangers in the temple, he is in conflict with them. He expresses his anger assertively at their activities.

We read about this event in John 2:14-17. When Jesus enters the temple, for him a sacred space, he finds it being corrupted by commercialism and consumerism. Neither anger nor rage is mentioned in the text, but his words and actions reveal his feelings. First, he chases the buyers and sellers out of the temple. Then he overturns the tables of the moneychangers. To those selling doves, the symbol of peace, he says, "Take these things away; stop making God's house a den of thieves." Then the disciples remember his words: "Zeal for your house will consume me." This is a poignant insight into the intensity of Jesus' anger at that moment. He has shown us the third way: active nonviolence.[6]

Anger Continuum

To help understand Jesus' anger here, let us look at the anger continuum I developed from an analysis of the interview data of a research project about anger. The people I interviewed indicated that they have different anger energies depending on the conflict situation, the people involved, and their own sense of what was happening. The different faces of this anger energy ranged from mild (frustration) to intense (rage), indicated by the two extremes of the continuum, with balanced anger energy in the middle. In the Figure below, the fluidity of this anger energy is visualized by the broken line. In some conflicts, there may be an intensification of anger energy from frustration to anger to rage; in other conflicts, a person's anger energy could begin with rage and move eventually to frustration. The interviewees stated that rage for them could be expressed nonviolently. In interpersonal conflicts, anger energy is interactive in a sort of cyclical fashion (rather than in a linear way, as the continuum might indicate). In a cosmic community context, interpersonal anger is interdependent. It is a fiery catalyst for growth.

FIGURE — ANGER CONTINUUM

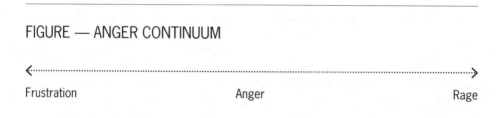

Frustration   Anger   Rage

Jesus' anger energy intensified when he saw others making "my house of prayer a den of thieves." He interrupted the desecration without causing physical harm to any of the people concerned. As David Augsburger explains, "Christ knew and exercised the emotion of anger. His anger was over principles of right and wrong, not over persons and personalities."[7]

Love of Enemy: Love Is the Key

A nonviolent way of life, a spirituality of nonviolence in transforming our anger energy brings us back to our discussion of love.

Prophets of Nonviolence Revisited

Think a moment about our other models of nonviolence who learned to love their enemy: Gandhi, in the apartheid of South Africa and the injustice of India; Etty Hillesum, in the death camps of Poland; Dorothy Day, with the government and church officials in the US; and Leonard Desroches, with the police, government, church officials and legal system in Canada. Each of these four people showed that they could only love their enemy if they loved themselves. Forgiveness is about loving the other as subject. Sallie McFague points out, "Jesus…made the classic subject-subjects statement when he said, 'Love your enemies'. Treat the person who is against you…as a subject, as someone deserving respect and care."[8]

Forgiveness means letting go of the notion of always being right, always being perfect, always being the offended. Our enemy reveals to us our own brokenness, our own fears, our own incompleteness. Desroches suggests that my enemy is constructed from the denied and detested aspects of the self – the unacceptable bad objects within – which are combined with the undesirable perceptions in others.[9] Part of the process of forgiveness may be admitting being wrong.

Forgiveness is our internal healing of violations arising from conflict and is an ongoing process. This forgiveness must always happen in order for self-healing to take place. Reconciliation, on the other hand, is interpersonal healing: what I call mutual forgiveness. Forgiveness is always possible; reconciliation is not. They are two distinct processes.

Reconciliation

What Is Reconciliation?

Reconciliation is mutual forgiveness: an interpersonal process in which the persons involved experience the mutuality, trust, safety, compassion and non-violence they need to be able to ask for and receive forgiveness from each other. There is a mutual desire to renew and rebuild the relationship. This is an inter-dependent and interconnected movement away from resentment, revenge and retaliation to mutual healing of hurts and a re-establishment of trust.

Reconciliation is the apex of communion and the epitome of community. In forgiving and being forgiven, we are reconnected in community. Community is a process and a journey that requires openness, listening-dialogue, respect, equality and reciprocity. Paul alludes to reconciliation as mutual forgiveness in Ephesians 4:32: "Be kind and tender-hearted to one another, and forgive one another...."

Conditions for Reconciliation

1. Interpersonal reconciliation requires a safe environment. (When there has been violence or another kind of serious violation, the restoration of the relationship may be neither prudent nor advisable.)

2. Reconciliation requires respect. The people involved must be able to respect each other in all their similarities and differences. Reconciliation requires honouring diversity.

3. Reconciliation requires the willingness to risk and trust the healing regenerative and transformative principles of our cosmic community.

"Leave Your Gift and …"

I conclude this discussion of reconciliation with the wonderful passage in Matthew 5:23-25 that notes Jesus' desire for both forgiveness and reconciliation, for right relationships. He says, "If you are on your way to the altar with your gift and there you *remember your neighbour* has something against you, leave your gift and go first, *be reconciled with your neighbour,* and then come and present your offering" (italics added).

When and wherever possible, we are asked to take the next step and go and *be reconciled with our neighbour.*

Dealing with Another's Anger

The Right to Be Angry

I have yet to meet a person who is totally comfortable with someone else's anger. What happens inside you when you experience another's anger energy? This may be how others feel in the face of your anger.

Accepting another's anger is a skill we learn by doing and is tied into learning how to express our own anger. As with conflict skills, it may feel like we are always doing it by the "seat of our pants." Some guidelines may help us deal with another's anger.

Guidelines

Step 1: Dealing with My Own Anger

When I have difficulty admitting I am angry and when I am not learning how to express my anger in assertive, constructive and nonviolent ways, I may be overcome by someone else's anger. I may need help to access my anger and express it in a healthy way.

Step 2: Listening

I respond to the other person as one adult to another in a stance of listening-dialogue. Listening is the key to receiving another's anger. Interfering with the other's communication with attempts to correct the facts, give my perspective, suggest the person calm down, can escalate the other's anger expression.

Step 3: Giving Self-reminders

As I listen to the other, I remind myself that anger is a form of communicating needs and that most anger responses last less than a minute.[10] The anger feedback has a beginning, a middle and an end. I remind myself not to interrupt, but to learn from what is said.

Step 4: Keeping Silence

Silence creates a sacred space for what has been shared and helps both parties breathe deeply, stay focused and think about what has been said. In our very verbal world, the immediate temptation is to fill silences with words that explain and justify. In receiving the anger of another, silence can be golden. When we sense we have been heard and that what we have said has been compassionately received, this creates an atmosphere for healing and moving on.

Step 5: Offering a Grounded, Nondefensive Response

When the time comes for me to respond, it is essential to stay grounded and respond as nondefensively, compassionately and yet as assertively as possible. To respond aggressively or violently just keeps the conflict going.

Step 6: Giving Follow-up to the Feedback

I may be able to respond immediately to the feedback given. I may discover the truth underneath all that has been shared, and see that I need to apologize. I may share in my feedback to the person that I have been misjudged and that what is needed is mutual forgiveness/reconciliation as subject to subject (not winner/loser). "It is difficult to dialogue with others if we cling arrogantly to the idea that we are right."[11] Or, I may ask for time (time out) to think about the anger received, suggesting another time to explore the issue together once I have had time to gain some perspective on it.

Exceptions

Accepting another's anger does not mean accepting abuse (verbal or physical) or violence of any kind. If I sense the person is becoming violent, I must ensure my own safety by removing myself from the situation. Even when I am on the telephone and the other becomes abusive, I simply say, "I hear lots of energy in your words and I would be more comfortable discussing this issue with you at another time. I am going to hang up now but I would be willing to discuss the matter when you are calmer." With that, I gently place the phone back in the receiver.

The Benefits of Anger

If you are patient in the moment of anger, you will
escape a hundred days of sorrow.

Chinese Proverb

Here is a brief overview of some of the benefits of intrapersonal and interpersonal anger in our lives. Take a moment to name some of the benefits of anger in your own life and then compare them with what follows.

Anger Increases Self-knowledge

Anger is a way of keeping me in touch with who I am at my deepest core. A God-given emotion, anger functions primarily as a signal that something is amiss. It goes hand in hand with fear as indicated in our fight/flight atavistic response. To help discover what this underlying emotion is, I can ask myself, "What would I be feeling right now, if I were not feeling angry?" I also find it helpful to do a bit of self-talk, asking myself whether I am overtired, stressed, coming down with a cold, etc. With such self-talk, I can gently take care of me and focus on the underlying issue or the intrapersonal anger, rather than what would appear to be an external cause.

Anger Offers a Catalyst for Growth

Anger, as with all the other emotions, physiologically generates significant energy to become a change catalyst. The body is prepared for action. When I analyze and interpret this energy, I find out what I am feeling and why. Its phenomenal energy, when it is used constructively, assertively and nonviolently, has a way of transforming us. Part of this transformation happens through forgiveness (spiritual healing), which has many benefits, including an increase in both physical and psychological health.[12]

Anger is a passion, a yearning for more. It challenges us in our lives to look at the here and now and to move towards conversion.

Anger Grounds Us in Gaia

Anger energy in its organic fluidity is the red in the rainbow of Gaia, keeping us grounded and connected to all life. Acknowledging anger's ebb and flow helps us recognize our interdependence and interconnectedness with all of creation so we may respect and love all life.

PART V: REFLECTION AND DISCUSSION STARTERS

1. Revisit the Five A's of anger transformation, highlighting the one(s) that you need to focus on.

2. How can the personal and professional "I" statements help you express anger?

3. How do you release your physical anger energy?

4. In the psychological expression of your anger, how can the "after," "before" and "during" strategies help? Which one(s) is the easiest/hardest for you? Why?

5. Forgiveness is the spiritual part of healthy anger energy transformation. Do you agree or disagree? Why?

6. "Forgive, but don't forget." What does this mean for you?

7. Forgiveness and reconciliation are two different processes. Discuss.

8. Forgiveness as a way of life (an attitude, a decision, a desire) is essential to dealing with anger nonviolently. Why?

9. Jesus' Third Way, with emphasis on love of our enemy, is very challenging. Discuss.

10. How can the guidelines for dealing with another's anger help you deal with anger nonviolently?

EPILOGUE

THE JOURNEY AHEAD

If we hesitate before each step we take,
we could spend our lives standing on one foot.

Chinese Proverb

Community: Alone, Together

It is consoling to see the journey ahead as a continuation of the small steps we have made throughout our lives. Reading and reflecting in these pages on such taboo topics as conflict and anger is an important step! The path of a spirituality of nonviolence transforms our intrapersonal and interpersonal conflict and anger. At times, our steps are sure and confident; at other times, they are tentative and discouraged. A cosmic community context offers support along the way.

We must embrace the pilgrimage aspect of this journey into wholeness, and love unconditionally the pilgrim part of ourselves. Changed by the pilgrimage, the spiritual quest, we come back to our everyday lives with a ray of hope that moves us into a future in ways we may never have imagined. As Jean Shinoda Bolen puts it in *Crossing to Avalon*, pilgrims "leave behind their usual lives and go in search of something (or someone) they are missing, not necessarily knowing what that is."[1]

Pilgrimage is not only a physical journey; it is also a psychological and spiritual one. We explore our innermost being as we open ourselves to risk, realizing that we have nothing to lose and everything to gain. It is a faith journey and a conversion process of profound inner emptying. There is no room for power over and control here. Esther de Waal reminds us in *The Celtic Way of Prayer,* "The openness of the 'peregrinato' should never tempt us to forget that without the still center, the journey, whether inner or outer, is impossible."[2]

The community dimension of pilgrimage is key – a union of minds, hearts and values such as we find in the mentors and prophets who challenge us. As a community, we journey with other pilgrims or mentors who have a vision of what "wholeness" looks like in this particular pilgrimage.

Pilgrimage Journey

On pilgrimage, we must grieve the secure, the familiar: the ways of being and doing in our old story, our old worldviews, are no longer useful as we build the reign of God and right relationships. Such a pilgrimage is a three-part process of encounter, passing over/coming back, and mapping the journey.[3] Despite the linear sense of this pilgrimage, it is also organic and fluid.

Encounter

Learning to deal nonviolently and creatively with our intrapersonal and interpersonal conflict and anger requires that we move away from the old and familiar story of our universe. In the openness and heart-availability necessary for pilgrimage, we encounter Gaia, Mother Earth, and a quantum universe, a cosmic community that respects all life forms. As co-creators, we encounter the sacred magnificence of this cosmic universe community. This encounter helps soften our hearts of stone to hearts of flesh (Ezekiel 36:26) so we may embrace our conflict and anger nonviolently. Part of this pilgrimage encounter involves emulating our prophets of nonviolence and following Jesus' Third Way. Essentially, the encounter is about our conversion to this way of life: our stepping away from anyone and anything that does not foster this new vision of right relationships and the new reign of compassion and justice.

Passing Over/Coming Back

As we enter into the mystery of this encounter, the passing over to this new way of life slowly and quietly follows. Here begins the crux of our pilgrimage of conversion to a life of nonviolence, the depth of moving from what we know about the Earth at an intellectual level to the actual experience. "Passing over is a shifting of standpoint, a going over to another culture, another way of life," says Ewert Cousins in *Christ of the 21st Century*.[4] We move away from the dominant Western culture that emphasizes power over, win/lose, and the misuse and abuse of the earth and all life species.

Essential to the passing over is the coming back. The Transfiguration (Matthew 17:1-7) is a gospel example of the part of us that wants to stay on the esoteric mountaintop – the rarefied experience of the retreat, the workshop, the conversion. Like Peter, James and John before us, we cannot build tents and stay up there: we must come down from the mountain; we must return to everyday life to live our conversion. We come back changed and humbly aware that things can never be the same for us. We must integrate this spirituality of nonviolence into the new story of the universe. "Passing over," continues Cousins, "leads to a... coming back with new insight into one's own culture, one's own way of life."[5]

Mapping the Journey

Mapping the journey helps us live out the stark reality that the only thing changed is ourselves. The challenge is to learn how to enflesh such changes in a world that is still violent, consumeristic and with quick fixes for dealing with conflict and anger. Once we are back in our own culture, in our own comfortable pew, many of us stop short of taking the final steps in our conversion transformation. In

Jean Vanier's words, "To enter into a new covenant, and belong to a new people, a community with new values, we have to leave another people.... This passage can be a very painful uprooting and usually takes a long time."[6]

It is important to keep telling ourselves that this transformation is possible but that there are no magic solutions. It is a lifetime pilgrimage and yet the pilgrimage of this present moment. How consoling. How do-able.

To help our integration process, we are called in various ways to map the journey. How you map your journey will be unique to you. Others have done so before us; we can follow the models they leave behind. Gandhi, Dorothy Day, Etty Hillesum, Leonard Desroches and Jesus are just a few prophetic models who can be soul friends for the journey.

Three Things I Ask

To conclude, let us explore the prophet Micah's invitation (6:8): "Only three things I ask of you: act justly, love tenderly and walk humbly with your God."

Act Justly

We act justly when we think globally and act locally, remembering the bigger picture of our cosmic home community. We take steps to protect and preserve the Earth, our home, for future generations. There is a certain discipline in living simply so others can simply live. This is all about nonviolence, learning when enough is enough. Learning to reduce, reuse and recycle, we clear out the clutter of our lives to provide a larger space for all life. Even more amazingly, we learn to love the true inner freedom such simplicity brings.

To act justly requires discipline. We must trust in the God of Wisdom that, for at least today, we will act out of a conviction of global eco-justice.

Love Tenderly

To love tenderly is to act justly to the extreme, loving our enemy both within ourselves and outside ourselves. It is all about a spirituality of nonviolence, both as a way of life and a strategy for dealing with our conflict and anger. By loving tenderly, we learn to forgive ourselves and others. It is essential to a full life.

Walk Humbly

Part of walking humbly is learning humility, as we recognize that we are part of a majestic whole: not the apex, but one of the many manifestations of the grandeur of God. We learn that we, with all life forms, are a community of subjects.

With Your God

Who is God for you? Our many faiths, religions and spiritualities are our human attempts to communicate with the divine in our lives. Each of us must discover and nurture the ineffable mystery that connects us to all others in our cosmic community.

Blessings on the journey. One day at a time, that is enough.

APPENDIX

PERSONAL ANGER ASSESSMENT SURVEY

Name: _____ Date: _____

DIRECTIONS:

1. Think of one particular person/situation in answering the following statements.

2. Answer each statement quickly with "YES" or "NO".

>   "YES" = "most of the time" or "usually"
>   "NO" = "seldom" or "never"

_____ 1. I am aware/admit when I a angry.

_____ 2. I let my anger build up until I finally explode.

_____ 3. I raise my voice/shout when I am angry.

_____ 4. I want to hit, slap, punch you when I am angry with you.

_____ 5. I blame myself when I am angry with you.

_____ 6. I am sarcastic when I am angry with you.

_____ 7. I curse/swear when I am angry with you.

_____ 8. I can state my needs when you and I have a difference of opinion.

_____ 9. I tend to get even when I have been hurt or disappointed.

_____ 10. I push, shove, hit you when we are in the heat of conflict.

_____ 11. I am ashamed when I get angry.

_____ 12. I can disagree with you without attacking you verbally or physically.

_____ 13. I feel powerless when I am angry.

_____ 14. I bang, break things when I am fed up/angry.

_____ 15. I tend to forget my obligations, commitments to you when I am angry with you.

_____ 16. I say "yes" when I really want to say "no" to you when we have a quarrel.

_____ 17. I tend to "punish" you by coming late/leaving early when you and I have had a fight.

_____ 18. I feel powerless in conflict situations with you.

_____ 19. I tend to let my anger fester inside to the point of becoming sad/dejected.

_____ 20. I avoid you, stop talking with you when I am hurt.

_____ 21. I vent my anger on someone safer when I am really upset with you.

_____ 22. I tend to be critical of you when I am disappointed with you.

_____ 23. I accept my anger as a clue that something is wrong.

_____ 24. I give you feedback about my being hurt in a conflict situation with you.

_____ 25. I tend to be negative and argumentative.

_____ 26. I see forgiveness as integral to dealing with my anger.

_____ 27. I am afraid of my anger.

_____ 28. I keep my cool when I am angry with you.

_____ 29. I pressure you to see/do things my way when we have a difference of opinion.

_____ 30. I want to be accepted so I agree with you no matter what.

_____ 31. I tend to get sick when I let my anger accumulate and fester.

_____ 32. I try to be open to your perspective when we see things differently.

MY ANGER RESPONSE STYLES SCORING SHEET

Name: _____ Date: _____

SCORING DIRECTIONS:

To determine your style, LOOK ONLY at the statements to which you responded "YES".

a) Circle the numbers below in each type to which you answered "YES".

b) Total your "YES" responses for each type.

SCORING:

TYPE	NUMBERS	TOTAL
1. PASSIVE	5, 11, 13, 16, 18, 19, 27, 30	_____
2. AGGRESSIVE	3, 4, 7, 10, 14, 22, 25, 29	_____
3. PASSIVE-AGGRESSIVE	2, 6, 9, 15, 17, 20, 21, 31	_____
4. ASSERTIVE	1, 8, 12, 23, 24, 26, 28, 32	_____

RESULTS:

The higher your total number of "YES" scores for a given type, the more likely this style is your usual style. You may also have a "back-up" style which you use when the other one "doesn't work." The next highest number or equal number of "YES" scores may be this back-up style.

a) My usual/most common anger response style is _____.

b) My back-up anger response style is _____.

RATIONALE:

There are 32 statements in this self-assessment, with 8 statements for each of the four communication styles learned from home, school, church, society: passive, aggressive, passive-aggressive and assertive. Each person uses all four styles; the passive, aggressive and passive-aggressive styles are violent and nonconstructive. The GOAL, with more awareness of one's particular anger style responses, is to move to an ASSERTIVE and NONVIOLENT ANGER RESPONSE STYLE, using "I" statements.

LIST OF TABLES AND FIGURES

NOTES

Chapter 1

1 Hazel Henderson. *Paradigms in Progress: Life Beyond Economics*. London: Adamantine Press, 1993, 134.

2 Kathleen Fischer. *Moving On: A Spirituality for Women of Maturity*. London: Red Books, 1996, 89.

3 Hazel Henderson. 1993, 72.

4 Sallie McFague. *The Body of God: An Ecological Theology*. London: SCM Press, 1993, 55.

5 Ursula Goodenough. *The Sacred Depths of Nature*. Oxford: Oxford University Press, 1998, 4.

6 Diarmuid O'Murchu. *Quantum Theology*. New York: Crossroad Publishing, 1997b, 184.

7 Mary Conrow Coelho. *Awakening Universe, Emergent Personhood*. Lima, OH: Wyndham Hall Press, 2002, 37.

8 Brian Swimme; Thomas Berry. *The Universe Story: From the Primordial Flaring Forth to the Ecozoic Era – A Celebration of the Unfolding of the Cosmos*. San Francisco: Harper San Francisco, 1992, 250.

9 Fritjof Capra; David Steindl-Rast. *Belonging to the Universe: Explorations on the Frontiers of Science and Spirituality*. San Francisco: Harper San Francisco, 1991, 139.

10 Peter Russell. *The Global Brain Awakes*. Palo Alto, CA: Global Brain, 1995, 149.

11 Hazel Henderson. 1993, 71.

12 Brian Swimme; Thomas Berry. 1992, 241.

13 Antoine de Saint Exupery. *The Little Prince*. Ware, UK: Wordsworth Editions, 1995 (1969, 1943), 66.

14 Antoine de Saint Exupery. 1995 (1969, 1943), 82.

15 C.S. Lewis. *The Four Loves*. London: Harper-Collins Publishers, 1960, 155.

16 Timothy P. Jackson. *The Priority of Love: Christian Charity and Social Justice*. Princeton, NJ: Princeton University Press, 2003, 10, 22.

17 Robert M. Augros; George N. Stanciu. *The New Story of Science: Mind and the Universe*. New York: Bantam Book, 1986, xiv, xv.

Chapter 2

1 William Robert Miller. *Nonviolence: A Christian Interpretation*. London: George Allen & Unwin, 1964, 24–25.

2 Leonard Desroches. *Allow the Water*. Toronto: Dunamis Publishers, 1996, 474–475.

3 Joyce L Hocker; William W. Wilmot. *Interpersonal Conflict* (Third Edition). Dubuque, IA: William C. Brown Publishers, 1991, 113.

4 Vern Neufeld Redekop. *From Violence to Blessing: How an Understanding of Deep-rooted Conflict Can Open Paths to Reconciliation.* Ottawa: Novalis, 2002, 21, 162–163.

5 Walter Wink. *The Powers That Be: Theology for the New Millennium.* New York: Galilee Doubleday, 1998, 46, 48.

6 Walter Wink. 1998, 68.

7 Carmen Germaine Warner. *Conflict Intervention in Social and Domestic Violence.* Bowie, MD: Robert J. Brady Company, 1981, 37.

8 Mitch Albom. *Tuesdays with Morrie.* London: Little, Brown and Company, 1999, 82–83.

9 Ernest Becker. *The Denial of Death.* New York: The Free Press, 1973, xii.

10 Kathleen Fischer. *Moving On: A Spirituality Journey for Women of Maturity.* London: Redwood Books, 1996, 66.

11 I. C. Sharma. The Ethics of Jainism, in, Robert Holmes (Ed.). *Nonviolence in Theory and Practice.* Belmont, CA: Wadsworth Publishing Company, 1990, 10.

12 Reuven Kimelman. Nonviolence in the Talmud, in, Robert Holmes (Ed.). *Nonviolence in Theory and Practice.* Belmont, CA: Wadsworth Publishing Company, 1990, 20.

13 Lawrence S. Apsey. How Transforming Power Has Been Used in the Past by Early Christians, in Robert Holmes (Ed.). *Nonviolence in Theory and Practice.* Belmont, CA: Wadsworth Publishing Company, 1990, 27–28.

14 "Advocates of the Just War theory support war if the war is waged in pursuit of justice, carried out with the right intention, undertaken by lawful authority, has a probability of success, is proportionate and discriminates between the innocent and military targets." Archbishop John Myers. *Origins*, Vol. 31, no. 24, November 22, 2001, 411.

15 Tom Harpur. *Would You Believe?* Toronto: McClelland & Stewart, 1996, 83.

16 Diarmuid O'Murchu. *Evolutionary Faith.* New York: Orbis, 2002.

17 Diarmuid O'Murchu. *Quantum Theology.* New York: Crossroad Publishing, 1997b.

18 Diarmuid O'Murchu. 1997b, 12.

19 Diarmuid O'Murchu. *Reclaiming Spirituality.* New York: Crossroad Publishing, 1997a, vii. And, Sallie McFague. Super, Natural Christians. Minneapolis: Fortress Press, 1997, 10.

20 Sandra Schneiders. Spirituality in the Academy, in, *Theological Studies*, 1989, 50, 4, 696.

Chapter 3

1 Walter Brueggemann. *The Prophetic Imagination.* Philadelphia: Fortress Press, 1978, 23.

2 Janet Malone. Prophets in Religious Life, in, *Human Development*, Fall, 2001.

3 Walter Brueggemann. 1978, 45.

4   Rosemary Haughton. *The Transformation of Man: A Study of Conversion and Community*. London: Geoffrey Chapman, 1967, 129, 131.

5   There are more men than women on this list because women's works are not recorded to the same extent that men's are. The lacuna has begun to be remedied; ongoing efforts to uncover prophetic women of nonviolence in history are still needed.

6   Louis Fischer. *Gandhi: His Life and Message for the World*. New York: A Mentor Book, 1954, 10.

7   Louis Fischer. 1954, 21.

8   Eileen Egan. *Peace Be With You: Justified Warfare or the Way of Nonviolence*. New York: Orbis Books, 1999, 199.

9   Robert Holmes (Ed.). *Nonviolence in Theory and Practice*. Belmont: CA: Wadsworth Publishing Company, 1990, 55.

10 Leonard Desroches. *Allow the Water*. Toronto: Dunamis Publishers, 1996, 474.

11 Louis Fischer. 1954, 15.

12 Louis Fischer. 1954, 29.

13 Louis Fischer. 1954, 18.

14 Walter Wink. *The Powers That Be: Theology for the New Millennium*. New York: Galilee Doubleday, 1998, 116.

15 Eileen Egan. 1999, 201.

16 Dorothy Day. *The Long Loneliness: The Autobiography of Dorothy Day*. New York: Harper and Brothers, Publishers, 1952, 87.

17 Dorothy Day. 1952, 264.

18 Dorothy Day. 1952, 141

19 Dorothy Day. 1952, 149–150.

20 Dorothy Day. 1952, 273.

21 Eileen Egan. 1999, 270.

22 Eileen Egan. 1999, 274.

23 Eileen Egan. 1999, 289.

24 Dorothy Day. *On Pilgrimage*. Grand Rapids, MI: William B. Eerdmans Publishing Company, 1999, 51.

25 Dorothy Day. 1999, 238–239.

26 Eileen Egan. 1999, 305.

27 Etty Hillesum. *Etty, A Diary 1941–1943*. (Jonathan Cape, Translator). London: Jonathan Cape Ltd., 1983, 26. [Canadian edition: Klaas A.D. Smelik (Ed.). Etty: The Letters and Diaries of Etty Hillesum 1941–1943. Ottawa: Novalis, 2002.]

28 Etty Hillesum. 1983, 121.

29 Etty Hillesum. 1983, 74, 77.

30 Etty Hillesum. 1983, 91.

31 Etty Hillesum. 1983, 26.

32 Etty Hillesum. 1983, 15.

33 Etty Hillesum. 1983, 47.

34 Etty Hillesum. 1983, 52.

35 Etty Hillesum. 1983, 72.

36 Etty Hillesum. 1983, 108.

37 Etty Hillesum. 1983, 81.

38 Etty Hillesum. 1983, 82.

39 Etty Hillesum. 1983, 110.

40 Etty Hillesum. 1983, 123.

41 Etty Hillesum. 1983, 127.

42 Etty Hillesum. 1983, 131.

43 Etty Hillesum. 1983, 149.

44 Etty Hillesum. 1983, 167.

45 Leonard Desroches. 1996, 22.

46 Leonard Desroches. 1996, 25.

47 Leonard Desroches. 1996, 26.

48 Leonard Desroches. 1996, 32.

49 Leonard Desroches. Who Is My Enemy?, *CRC Bulletin*, Winter 2000, 1.

50 Leonard Desroches. *Love of Enemy: The Cross and Sword Trial*. Ottawa: Dunamis Publishers, 2002, 2.

51 Leonard Desroches. 2002, 3.

52 Leonard Desroches. 2002, 39.

53 Leonard Desroches. 2002, 33.

54 Leonard Desroches. 2002, 32.

55 Leonard Desroches. 2000, 2.

56 Leonard Desroches. 1996, 31.

57 Leonard Desroches. 1996, 39.

58 Leonard Desroches. 1996, 66.

59 Leonard Desroches. 2002, 7.

60 Leonard Desroches. 1996, 119–120.

61 Leonard Desroches. 1996, 37.

62 Walter Wink in Leonard Desroches. 1996, 34.

63 Joseph Phelps. *More Light, Less Heat: How Dialogue Can Transform Christian Conflicts into Growth.* San Francisco: Jossey-Bass Publishers, 1999, 137.

64 Eileen Egan. 1999.

65 Walter Wink. 1998, 99, 103.

66 Eileen Egan. 1999, 155.

Chapter 4

1   Raymond W. Mack; Richard C. Snyder. The Analysis of Social Conflict – Toward an Overview and Synthesis, in, *Conflict Resolution Through Communication.* Fred E. Jandt (Ed.). New York: Harper & Row Publishers, 1973, 26.

2   Jacob Bercovitch. *Social Conflicts and Third Parties: Strategies of Conflict Resolution.* Boulder, CO: Westview Press, 1984, xi.

3   Louis Kriesberg. *The Sociology of Social Conflicts.* Englewood Cliffs, NJ: Prentice-Hall, 1973.

4   Jean Baker Miller. *Toward a New Psychology of Women.* Boston: Beacon Press, 1976, 125.

5   Wendy Grant. *Resolving Conflicts: How to Turn Conflict into Co-operation.* Rockport, MA: Element Books, 1997, 22.

6   Gini Graham Scott. *Conflicts with Others and Within Yourself.* Oakland, CA: New Harbinger Publishing, 1990, 40.

7   Joseph P. Folger; Marshall Scott Poole. *Working through Conflict: A Communication Perspective.* Palo Alto, CA: Scott, Foresman and Company, 1984, 7.

8   Joyce L. Hocker; William W. Wilmot. *Interpersonal Conflict* (Third Edition). Dubuque, IA: William C. Brown Publishers, 1991, 34.

9   Richard E. Walton. *Interpersonal Peacemaking: Confrontation and Third-Party Consultation.* Reading, MA: Addison-Wesley Publishing Company, 1969, 3.

10 Alan R Beals; Bernard J. Siegel. *Divisiveness and Social Conflict: An Anthropological Approach.* Stanford, CA: Stanford University Press, 1966, 20.

11 W. Barnett Pearce; Stephen W. Littlejohn. *Moral Conflict: When Social Worlds Collide.* London: Sage Publications, 1997, 68.

12 Joseph P. Folger; Marshall Scott Poole. 1984, 44.

13 Jeffrey Z. Rubin. Conflict from a Psychological Perspective, in, *Negotiation: Strategies for Mutual Gain.* Livinia Hall (Ed.). London: Sage Publications, 1993, 132.

14 Louis Kriesberg. 1973, 7.

15 David Cormack. *Peacing Together: From Conflict to Reconciliation.* Eastbourne, UK: Monarch Publications, 1989.

16 Speed Leas. *Moving Your Church Through Conflict.* Augsberger Press, 1985.

17 Joyce L. Hocker; William W. Wilmot. 1991, 193.

Chapter 5

1   Terence E. Deal. Cultural Change: Opportunity, Silent Killer or Metamorphosis? in, *Gaining Control of the Corporate Culture*. R. Kilmann; M. Saxton; R. Serpa (Eds.). San Francisco: Jossey-Bass, 1985, 300–301.

2   E. Franklin Dukes. *Resolving Public Conflict: Transforming Community and Governance*. New York: Manchester University Press, 1996, 127.

3   Martin Eggleton; David Trafford. *At Cross Purposes: Handling Conflict in the Church*. London: Stanley L. Hunt Printers, 2000, 17.

4   Joan Chittister. *The Fire in These Ashes*. Kansas City, MO: Sheed & Ward, 1995, 46.

5   Kristine C. Brewer. *Managing Stress*. UK: Gower Publishing, 1997, 35.

6   Kristine C. Brewer. 1997, 3.

7   Kristine C. Brewer. 1997, 3.

8   Kristine C. Brewer. 1997.

9   Nathaniel Branden. *A Woman's Self-Esteem: Stories of Struggle, Stories of Triumph*. San Francisco: Jossey-Bass Publishers, 1998, 8, 3–4.

10 Wendy Grant. *Resolving Conflicts: How to Turn Conflict into Co-operation*. Rockport, MA: Element Books, 1997, 24.

11 Janet Malone. Women and Self-Esteem, in, *Human Development*. Summer 1996, 5–7.

12 Nathaniel Branden. 1998, 8, 97.

13 Janet Malone. 1996, 5–7.

14 Alan Houel; Christian Godefoy. *How to Cope with Difficult People*. London: Sheldon Press, 1994, 83.

15 Carol Tavris; Carole Offir. *The Longest War: Sex Differences in Perspective*. San Francisco: Harcourt Brace Jovanovich, 1977.

16 Fran Ferder. *Words Made Flesh: Scripture, Psychology and Human Communication*. Notre Dame: Ave Maria Press, 1986, 142.

17 Carol Tavris; Carole Offir. 1977, 194.

18 Joan Chittister. *Heart of Flesh: A Feminist Spirituality for Women and Men*. Ottawa: Novalis, 1998, 79.

19 Joyce L. Hocker; William W. Wilmot. *Interpersonal Conflict* (Third Edition). Dubuque, IA: William C. Brown Publishers, 1991, 72.

20 *The Times* (London). May 26, 2003, 6.

21 *Origins*. March 20, 1997, 633.

22 *The Times*. May 26, 2003, 6.

23 *The Times*. May 26, 2003, 6.

24 *The Times*. May 26, 2003, 6.

25 *The Times.* May 26, 2003, 6.

26 *The Times.* May 26, 2003, 6.

27 Richard C. Weber. The Group: A Cycle from Birth to Death, in, *NTL Reading Book for Human Relations Training.* (Seventh Edition). Lawrence Porter; Bernard Mohr (Eds.). Arlington, VA: NTL Institute Publications Department, 1982, 68.

Chapter 6

1   Wendy Grant. *Resolving Conflicts: How to Turn Conflict into Cooperation.* Rockport, MA: Element Books, 1997.

2   William L. Ury; Jeanne M. Brett; Stephen B. Goldberg. *Getting Disputes Resolved: Designing Systems to Cut the Costs of Conflict.* London: Jossey-Bass Publishers, 1988, 38.

3   Kevin Avruch. *Culture and Conflict Resolution.* Washington, DC: United States Institute of Peace Press, 1998, 25, 101.

4   Kevin Avruch. 1998, 26.

5   W. Barnett Pearce; Stephen W. Littlejohn. *Moral Conflict: When Social Worlds Collide.* London: Sage Publications, 1997, 7.

6   Carolyn Schrock-Shenk. Introducing Conflict and Conflict Transformation, in, Carolyn Schrock-Shenk; Lawrence Ressler (Eds.). *Making Peace with Conflict: Practical Skills for Conflict Transformation.* Waterloo, ON: Herald Press, 1999, 35–36.

7   David Augsburger. *Caring Enough to Confront: Learning to Speak the Truth in Love.* Bassingstoke, UK: Marshall, Herald Press, 1985, 10–11.

8   Joseph Phelps. *More Light, Less Heat: How Dialogue Can Transform Christian Conflicts into Growth.* San Francisco: Jossey-Bass Publishers, 1999, 9.

9   Joseph Phelps. 1999, 20.

10 Paulo Freire. *Pedagogy of the Oppressed.* London: Penguin Books, 1993, 68.

11 Harriet Goldhor Lerner. *The Dance of Connection.* London: Piatkus Publishers, 2001, 203.

12 Ronald J. Fisher. *Interactive Conflict Resolution.* Syracuse: Syracuse University Press, 1997, 7.

13 Deborah M. Kolb. Her Place at the Table: Gender and Negotiation, in, *Negotiation: Strategies for Mutual Gain.* Lavinia Hall (Ed.). London: Sage Publications, 1993, 144.

14 W. Barnett Pearce; Stephen W. Littlejohn. 1997, 78–79.

15 Joseph Phelps. 1999, 26.

16 Martin Eggleton; David Trafford. *At Cross Purposes: Handling Conflict in the Church.* London: Stanley L. Hunt Printers, 2000, 3.

Chapter 7

1   Luis Pinzon; Nestor Valero-Silva. *A Proposal for a Critique of Contemporary Mediation Techniques: The Satisfaction Story.* Hull, UK: The University of Hull, 1996.

2   William L. Ury; Jeanne M. Brett; Stephen B. Goldberg. *Getting Disputes Resolved: Designing Systems to Cut the Costs of Conflict.* London: Jossey-Bass Publishers, 1988, 49.

3   Mark S. Umbreit. *Mediating Interpersonal Conflicts: A Pathway to Peace.* West Concord, MN: CPI Publishing, 1995, 5.

4   Jane Vella. *Learning to Listen, Learning to Teach.* San Francisco: Jossey-Bass Publishers, 1994, 59.

5   Paolo Freire. *Pedagogy of the Oppressed.* New York: Continuum, 1987, 54.

6   Ronald J. Fisher. *Interactive Conflict Resolution.* Syracuse: Syracuse University Press, 1997, 7–8.

7   Lewis Coser. *The Functions of Conflict.* New York: The Free Press, 1956, 47.

8   Lewis Coser. 1956, 38.

Chapter 8

1   James R. Averill. *The Acquisition of Emotions during Adulthood. The Social Construction of Emotions.* Ron Harre (Ed.). New York: Basil Blackwell, 1986.

2   Williard Gaylin. *The Rage Within: Anger in Modern Life.* New York: Simon & Schuster, 1984, 50.

3   Carl Georg Lange; William James (Eds.). *The Emotions.* New York: Hafner Publishing Company, 1967, 64.

4   Williard Gaylin. 1984, 10, 20–21.

5   Carol Tavris. *Anger: The Misunderstood Emotion.* New York: Simon & Schuster, 1982.

6   Susan Balfour. *Managing Stress in a Changing World.* UK: Gower Publishing, 1997, 56.

7   Carroll E. Izard. *Patterns of Emotions: A New Analysis of Anxiety and Depression.* New York: Academic Press, 1972.

8   Nathaniel Branden. *A Woman's Self-esteem: Stories of Struggle, Stories of Triumph.* San Francisco: Jossey-Bass Publishers, 1998, 81.

9   David Augsburger. *The Freedom of Forgiveness.* Bucks, UK: Scripture Press, 1989.

10 Harriet Goldhor Lerner. *The Dance of Anger.* New York: Pandora Press, HarperCollins, 1989, 1.

11 Harriet Goldhor Lerner. 1989, 4.

12 Gael Lindenfield. *Managing Anger.* London: Thorsons, 1993, 30.

13 Richard B. Gregg. *The Power of Nonviolence.* London: James Clarke & Company, 1960, 50.

14 Gael Lindenfield. 1993, 66.

Chapter 9

1   Carol Tavris. *Anger: The Misunderstood Emotion.* New York: Simon & Schuster, 1982, 33.

2   Magda B. Arnold. *Emotion and Personality. Volume I, Psychological Aspects.* New York: Columbia University Press, 1960, 256.

3   Carol Tavris. 1982, 22.

4   Adrian Faupel; Elizabeth Herrick; Peter Sharp. *Anger Management: A Practical Guide.* London: David Fulton Publishing, 1998, 10.

5   James R. Averill. *Anger and Aggression: An Essay on Emotion.* New York: Springer-Verlag, 1982, 317; 1986.

6   Teresa Bernardez. Women and Anger – Cultural Prohibitions and the Feminist Ideal, in, *Work in Progress.* Wellesley, MA: Stone Center Working Papers Series, 1988.

7   Jean Baker Miller. *Toward A New Psychology of Women.* Boston: Beacon Press, 1976.

8   Raymond W. Novaco. *Anger Control: The Development and Evaluation of an Experimental Treatment.* Lexington, MA: D.C. Heath and Company, 1975.

9   David Viscott. *The Language of Feelings.* New York: Pocket Books, 1976.

10 Stanlee Phelps; Nancy Austin. *The Assertive Woman.* San Francisco: Impact Publishers, 1975.

11 Roy Franklin Richardson. *The Psychology and Pedagogy of Anger.* Baltimore: Warwick and York, 1981.

12 Carol Tavris. 1982, 94.

13 Adrian Faupel; Elizabeth Herrick; Peter Sharp. 1998, 69.

14 Tim La Haye; Bob Phillips. *Anger Is a Choice.* UK: Marshall Morgan & Scott, 1985, 72.

15 David Augsburger. *Caring Enough to Confront: Learning to Speak the Truth in Love.* Bassing Stoke, UK: Marshall, Herald Press, 1985, 26.

16 Deborah Tannen. *That's Not What I Meant.* New York: Ballantine Books, 1986. And, *You Just Don't Understand.* New York: Ballatine Books, 1990. And, *Talking From 9 to 5.* New York: Avon Books, 1995.

17 Tim LaHaye; Bob Phillips. 1985. And, Janet Malone. Improving Your Expression of Anger, in, *Human Development,* Winter 1996, 26–29.

18 Gael Lindenfield. *Managing Anger.* London: Thorsons, 1993.

19 Robert Bolton. *People Skills.* New York: Touchstone, 1986, 123.

20 David W. Johnson. *Reaching Out: Interpersonal Effectiveness and Self-actualization.* (Seventh Edition). Toronto: Allyn and Bacon, 2000, 320.

21 Janet Malone. Winter 1996.

Chapter 10

1   Janet Malone. Winter 1996.

2   David W. Johnson. *Reaching Out: Interpersonal Effectiveness and Self-actualization.* (Seventh Edition). Toronto: Allyn and Bacon, 2000, 316.

3   David Augsburger. *Caring Enough to Confront: Learning to Speak the Truth in Love.* Bassing Stoke, UK: Marshall, Herald Press, 1985, 42.

4   Nathaniel Branden. *A Woman's Self-Esteem: Stories of Struggle, Stories of Triumph.* San Francisco: Jossey-Bass Publishers, 1998, 41.

5   David W. Johnson. *Reaching Out: Interpersonal Effectiveness and Self-actualization.* (Seventh Edition). Toronto: Allyn and Bacon, 2000.

6   Harriet Goldhor Lerner. *The Dance of Connection.* London: Piatkus Publishers Ltd., 2001, 235.

7   Ann Sutton. *Thriving on Stress.* Transatlantic Publications, 2000, 124.

Chapter 11

1   Michael E. McCullough; Kenneth E. Pargament; Carl E. Thoresen. The Psychology of Forgiveness, in Michael E. McCullough et al. (Eds.), *Forgiveness: Theory, Research, Practice.* New York: The Guilford Press, 2000, 9.

2   Kathleen Fischer. *Moving On: A Spirituality Journey for Women of Maturity.* London: Redwood Books, 1996, 132.

3   Gillian Stokes. *Forgiveness: Wisdom from Around the World.* London: MQ Publications, Limited, 2002, 26, 47.

4   Maria Harris. *Proclaim Jubilee.* Louisville, KY: Westminster John Knox Press, 1996, 51.

5   Kathleen Fischer. *Moving On: A Spirituality Journey for Women of Maturity.* London: Redwood Books, 1996, 130.

6   William H. Shannon. *Seeds of Peace.* New York: Crossroad Publishers, 1996, 104.

7   David Augsburger. *The Freedom of Forgiveness.* Bucks, UK: Scripture Press, 1989, 64.

8   Sallie McFague. *Super, Natural Christians: How We Should Love Nature.* Minneapolis: Fortress Press, 1997, 41.

9   Leonard Desroches. "Who Is My Enemy?" *CRC Bulletin*, Winter 2000.

10 James R. Averill. *Anger and Aggression: An Essay on Emotion.* New York: Springer-Verlag, 1982.

11 Jean Vanier. *Finding Peace.* Toronto: House of Anansi Press Inc., 2003, 16.

12 Mark S. Rye et al., Religious Perspectives on Forgiveness, in Michael E. McCullough et al. (eds). *Forgiveness: Theory, Research, Practice.* New York: The Guilford Press, 2000, 259.

Epilogue

1   Jean Shinoda Bolen. *Crossing to Avalon: A Woman's Midlife Pilgrimage.* New York: HarperCollins, 1994, 33.

2   Esther deWaal. *The Celtic Way of Prayer.* New York: Image Books, Doubleday, 1997, 9.

3   Ewert H. Cousins. *Christ of the 21st Century.* Rockport, MA: Element Books, 1992.

4   Ewert H. Cousins. 1992, 107.

5   Ewert H. Cousins. 1992, 107.

6   Jean Vanier. *Community and Growth: Our Pilgrimage Together.* New York: Paulist Press, 1979, 39.

BIBLIOGRAPHY

Adair, Margo and Sharon Howell. "Women Weave Community," in *Circles of Strength*, Helen Forsey, ed. Gabriola Island, BC: New Society Publishers, 1993, 35–41.

Albom, Mitch. *Tuesdays with Morrie*. London: Little, Brown and Company, 1999.

Amadeo, Linda and James J. Gill. "Managing Anger, Hostility and Aggression," in *Human Development*, Fall, 1980, 38–46.

Apsey, Lawrence S. "How Transforming Power Has Been Used in the Past by Early Christians," in *Nonviolence in Theory and Practice*, Robert Holmes, ed. Belmont, CA: Wadsworth, 1990, 27–28.

Arnold, Magda B. *Emotion and Personality*, Volume I: Psychological Aspects. New York: Columbia University Press, 1960.

———. *Emotion and Personality*, Volume II: Neurological and Physiological Aspects. New York: Columbia University Press, 1960.

Augros, Robert M. and George N. Stanciu. *The New Story of Science: Mind and the Universe*. New York: Bantam Books, 1986.

Augsburger, David. *Caring Enough to Confront: Learning to Speak the Truth in Love*. Bassing Stoke, UK: Marshall, Herald Press, 1985.

———. *The Freedom of Forgiveness*. Bucks, UK: Scripture Press, 1989.

———. *Conflict Mediation Across Cultures*. Louisville, KY: John Knox Press, 1992.

———. *Helping People to Forgive*. Louisville, KY: John Knox Press, 1996.

Averilll, James R. *Anger and Aggression: An Essay on Emotion*. New York: Springer-Verlag, 1982.

———. "The Acquisition of Emotions During Adulthood," in *The Social Construction of Emotions*, Ron Harre, ed. New York: Basil Blackwell, 1986, 98–118.

Avruch, Kevin. *Culture and Conflict Resolution*. Washington, DC: United States Institute of Peace Press, 1998.

Balfour, Susan. *Managing Stress in a Changing World*. UK: Gower, 1997.

Banet, Anthony G., Jr. "Yin/Yang: A Perspective on Theories of Group Development," in *Human Interaction and Group Development*, Don Carew, ed. NTL Reading Book, 1976, 61–76.

Baron, Anthony. *Violence in the Workplace*. Ventura, CA: Pathfinding Publishing, 1993.

Beals, Alan R. and Bernard J. Siegel. *Divisiveness and Social Conflict: An Anthropological Approach*. Stanford, CA: Stanford University Press, 1966.

Becker, Ernest. *The Denial of Death*. New York: The Free Press, 1973.

Belenky, Mary Field, Blythe McVicker Clinchy, Nancy Rule Goldberger and Jill Mattuck Tarule. *Women's Ways of Knowing: The Development of Self, Voice and Mind*. New York: Basic Books, 1986.

Belgrave, Bridget. "Communication That Simply Works (Nonviolent Communication, NVC)," in *Organisations and People*, 1998, 5, 3, 27–32.

Bellah, Robert N., Richard Madsen, William M. Sullivan, Ann Swidler and Steven M. Tipton. *Habits of the Heart: Individualism, and Commitment in American Life*. (Updated Edition). Berkley: University of California Press, 1996 (1985).

Benne, Kenneth D. "The Significance of Human Conflict," in *NTL Reading Book for Human Relations Training* (Seventh Edition). Lawrence Porter and Bernard Mohr, eds. Arlington, VA: NTL Publications Department, 1982, 58–61.

Bennis, Warren G. and Herbert A. Shepard. "A Theory of Group Development, Human Interaction and Group Dynamics: Supplemental Readings," in *NTL Reading Book*, Don Carew, ed. Arlington, VA: NTL Institute, 1976, 48–60.

Bennis, Warren and Burt Nanus. *Leaders: The Strategies for Taking Charge*. New York: Harper & Row, 1985.

Bercovitch, Jacob. *Social Conflicts and Third Parties: Strategies of Conflict Resolution*. Boulder, CO: Westview Press, 1984.

Bernardez, Teresa. "Women and Anger – Cultural Prohibitions and the Feminine Ideal," in *Work in Progress*. Wellesley, MA: Stone Center Working Papers Series, 1988.

Berry, Thomas. "The Universe, the University and the Ecozoic Era," in *Doors of Understanding: Conversations in Global Spirituality, in Honor of Ewert Cousins*, Steven Chase, ed. Quincy, IL: Franciscan Press, 1997, 80–95.

———. "Christianity's Role in the Earth Project," in *Christianity and Ecology: Seeking the Well-being of Earth and Humans*, Hessel and Ruether, eds. Cambridge: Harvard University Press, 2000, 127–134.

Best, Marion. "The Ecumenical Decade to Overcome Violence: Churches Seeking Reconciliation and Peace," in *Ecumenism*, September 2001, 5–9.

Bilodeau, Lorraine. *The Anger Workbook*. Minneapolis: Compcare, 1992.

Blake, Robert R. and Jane Srygley Mouton. "The Fifth Achievement," in *Conflict Resolution Through Communication*, E. Fred, ed. New York: Harper & Row, 1973, 88–102.

Bobbitt, Philip. *The Shield of Achilles: War, Peace & the Course of History*. London: Allen Lane, The Penguin Press, 2002.

Bolman, Lee G. and Terrence E. Deal. *Modern Approaches to Understanding and Managing Organisations*. San Francisco: Jossey-Bass, 1985.

Bolton, Robert. *People Skills*. New York: Touchtone, 1986.

Boulding, Kenneth E. *Conflict and Defense: A General Theory*. New York: Harper & Row, 1962.

———. "Conflict Management as a Learning Process," in *Conflict in Society*, Anthony de Rueck and Julie Knight, eds. London: J & A Churchill, 1966, 236–248.

———. *Three Faces of Power*. London: Sage, 1990.

Bourne, Peter G. (ed.). *The Psychology and Physiology of Stress*. New York: Academic Press, 1969.

Branden, Nathaniel. *A Woman's Self-Esteem: Stories of Struggle, Stories of Triumph*. San Francisco: Jossey-Bass, 1998.

Brewer, Kristine C. *Managing Stress*. UK: Gower, 1997.

Brownwell, Baker. *The Human Community: Its Philosophy & Practice for a Time of Crisis*. New York: Harper & Brothers, 1950.

Brueggemann, Walter. *The Prophetic Imagination*. Philadelphia: Fortress Press, 1978.

———. *Revelation and Violence: A Study in Contextualization*. Milwaukee: Marquette University Press, 1986.

———. *The Threat of Life: Sermons on Pain, Power and Weakness*. Charles Campbell, ed. Minneapolis: Augsburg Press, 1996.

Burtt, E.A. (ed.). *The Teachings of the Compassionate Buddha*. New York: The New American Library, 1955.

Campbell, Anne. *Men, Women and Aggression*. New York: HarperCollins, Basic Books, 1993.

Capra, Fritjof. *The Tao of Physics*. Bungay, Suffolk: The Chaucer Press, 1975.

Capra, Fritjof and David Steindl-Rast. *Belonging to the Universe: Explorations on the Frontiers of Science and Spirituality*. San Francisco: Harper San Francisco, 1991.

Carrington, Patricia. *The Power of Letting Go*. London: Vega, 2001.

Carlson, Dwight L. *Overcoming Hurts and Anger*. Eugene, OR: Harvest House, 1981.

Casarjian, Robin. *Forgiveness: A Bold Choice for a Peaceful Heart*. New York: Bantam Books, 1992.

Chase, Steven (ed.). *Doors of Understanding: Conversations in Global Spirituality in Honor of Ewert Cousins*. Quincy, IL: Franciscan Press, 1997.

Chittister, Joan. *Woman Strength: Modern Church, Modern Women*. Kansas City, MO: Sheed & Ward, 1990.

———. *The Fire in These Ashes*. Kansas City, MO: Sheed & Ward, 1995.

———. *Heart of Flesh: A Feminist Spirituality for Women and Men*. Ottawa: Novalis, 1998.

Chopra, Deepak. *How to Know God: The Soul's Journey into the Mystery of Mysteries*. London: Rider, 2000.

Clark, David. *Basic Communities: Towards an Alternative Society*. London: SPCK, 1977.

Clark, Stephen R. L. *How to Think About the Earth: Philosophical and Theological Models in Ecology*. New York: Mowbray, 1993.

CMSM (Conference of Major Superiors of Men). *Shalom Strategy: A Manual to Promote Nonviolence, Reconciliation and Peacemaking*. Washington, DC: 1996.

Cobb, Larry R. and Ann N. Dapice. "The Conditions for Creative Social Conflict: The Works of Mary Parker Follett," in *Religion and Philosophy in the United States of America*, Vol. I, Peter Freese, ed. Germany: Heiskllung, 1987, 95–110.

Cormack, David. *Peacing Together: From Conflict to Reconciliation*. Eastbourne, UK: Monarch Publications, 1989.

Cornelius, K. Helena and Shoshana Faire. *Everyone Can Win*. New York: Simon & Schuster, 1987.

Coser, Lewis A. *The Functions of Conflict*. New York: The Free Press, 1956.

————. *Continuities in the Study of Conflict*. New York: The Free Press, 1967.

Cousins, Ewert H. *Christ of the 21ˢᵗ Century*. Rockport, MA: Element, 1992.

Crum, Thomas F. *The Magic of Conflict*. New York: Simon & Schuster, 1987.

Curle, Adam. *Tools for Transformation: A Personal Study*. UK: Hawthorn Press, 1990.

Dana, Daniel. *Talk It Out: 4 Steps to Managing People Problems in Your Organisation*. London: Kogan Page, 1990.

Dana, Daniel. *Managing Differences: How to Build Better Relationships at Work and Home* (Second Edition). Overland Park, KS: MTI Publications, 1999.

Davison, Brenda. *What's All This About Stress?* Liverpool, UK: Tudor, 1999.

Day, Dorothy. *The Long Loneliness: The Autobiography of Dorothy Day*. New York: Harper and Brothers, 1952.

————. *On Pilgrimage*. Grand Rapids, MI: William B. Eerdmans, 1999.

Deal, Terrence E. "Cultural Change: Opportunity, Silent Killer, or Metamorphosis?" in *Gaining Control of the Corporate Culture*, R. Kilmann, M. Saxton and R. Serpa, eds. San Francisco: Jossey-Bass, 1985, 192–331.

Deal, Terrence E. and Allan A. Kennedy. *Corporate Cultures: The Rites and Rituals of Corporate Life*. Reading, MA: Addison-Wesley, 1982.

Deetz, Stanley A. and Sheryl Stevenson. *Managing Interpersonal Communication*. New York: Harper & Row, 1986.

Delanty, Gerard. *Community*. London: Routledge, 2003.

de Rueck, Anthony and Julie Knight (eds.). *Conflict in Society*. London: J & A Churchill, 1966.

de Saint Exupery, Antoine. *The Little Prince*. Ware, UK: Wordsworth Editions, 1995, (1969, 1943).

de Waal, Esther. *The Celtic Way of Prayer*. New York: Image Books, Doubleday, 1997.

Desroches, Leonard. *Allow the Water*. Toronto: Dunamis, 1996.

————. *Love of Enemy: The Cross and Sword Trial*. Ottawa: Dunamis, 2002.

————. *Spiritualité et pratique de la nonviolence*. Ottawa: Novalis, 2004.

Deutsch, Morton. "Conflicts: Productive and Destructive," in *Conflict Resolution Through Communication*, Fred E. Jandt, ed. New York: Harper & Row, 1973, 155–197.

Douglass, James W. *The Non-violent Cross: A Theology of Resolution and Peace*. New York: MacMillan, 1968.

Downey, Michael. *Understanding Christian Spirituality*. Mahwah, NJ: Paulist Press, 1997.

Dukes, E. Franklin. *Resolving Public Conflict: Transforming Community and Governance*. New York: Manchester University Press, 1996.

The Ecumenist. "Churches Seeking Reconciliation and Peace: The World Council of Churches' Decade to Overcome Violence." Summer 2000, 1–5.

Egan, Eileen. *Peace Be With You: Justified Warfare or the Way of Nonviolence*. New York: Orbis Books, 1999.

Eggleton, Martin and David Trafford. *At Cross Purposes: Handling Conflict in the Church*. London: Stanley L. Hunt, 2000.

Eliot, T. S. *Four Quartets*. London: Faber and Faber, 1944.

Ellis, Albert. *Anger: How to Live With and Without It*. Secausus, NJ: Citadel Press, 1977.

Faupel, Adrian, Elizabeth Herrick and Peter Sharp. *Anger Management: A Practical Guide*. London: David Fulton, 1998.

Ferder, Fran. *Words Made Flesh: Scripture, Psychology and Human Communication*. Notre Dame: Ave Maria Press, 1986.

Ferguson, Marilyn. *The Aquarian Conspiracy: Personal and Social Transformation in the 1980s*. Los Angeles: J. P. Tarcher, 1980.

Fischer, Kathleen. *Women at the Well: Feminist Perspectives on Spiritual Direction*. New York: Paulist Press, 1988.

———. *Moving On: A Spirituality Journey for Women of Maturity*. London: Redwood Books, 1996.

———. *Transforming Fire: Women Using Anger Creatively*. New York: Paulist Press, 1999.

Fischer, Louis. *Gandhi: His Life and Message for the World*. New York: A Mentor Book, 1954.

Fisher, B. Aubrey. "The Pragmatic Perspective of Communication," in *Human Communication Theory*, Frank F. X. Dance, ed. New York: Harper & Row, 1980 (a), 172–219.

———. *Small Group Decision Making*. New York: McGraw Hill, 1980 (b).

Fisher, B. Aubrey and Leonard Hawes. "An Interact System Model: Generating a Grounded Theory of Small Groups," in *Quarterly Journal of Speech*, 1971, 57, 444–453.

Fisher, Robert E. *Quick to Listen, Slow to Speak*. Wheaton, IL: Wheaton Books, 1987.

Fisher, Roger and William Ury. *Getting to Yes: Negotiating Agreement Without Giving In*. Markham, ON: Penguin Books, 1983.

Fisher, Roger and Scott Brown. *Getting Together*. Boston: Houghton Mifflin, 1988.

Fisher, Ronald J. *Interactive Conflict Resolution*. Syracuse: Syracuse University Press, 1997.

Folger, Joseph P. and Marshall Scott Poole. *Working Through Conflict: A Communication Perspective*. Palo Alto, CA: Scott, Foresman and Company, 1984.

Folger, Joseph P., Marshall Scott Poole and Randall K. Stutman. *Working Through Conflict: Strategies for Relationships, Groups and Organizations* (Third Edition). New York: Longman, 1997.

Forsey, Helen (ed.). *Circles of Strength*. Gabriola Island, BC: New Society Publishers, 1993.

Forsey, Helen. "Regenerating Community: An Introduction," in *Circles of Strength*, Gabriola Island, BC: New Society Publishers, 1993, 1–9.

Fox, Matthew. *A Spirituality Named Compassion and the Healing of the Global Village, Humpty Dumpty and Us*. Minneapolis: Winston Press, 1979.

———. *Creation Spirituality: Liberating Gifts for the Peoples of the Earth*. San Francisco: Harper San Francisco, 1991.

Frank, F. X. (ed.). *Human Communication Theory*. New York: Harper & Row, 1980.

Fransella, Fay and Kay Frosk. *On Being a Woman: A Review of Research on How Women See Themselves*. London: Tavistock, 1977.

Freire, Paulo. *Pedagogy of the Oppressed*. London: Penguin Books, 1993.

Fromm, Eric in *A Matter of Life*, Clara Urquhart, ed. London: Jonathan Cape, 1963.

Gandhi, Mahatma. *All Men Are Brothers: Autobiographical Reflections*. New York: Continuum, 1984.

Gangadean, Ashok K. "Dialogical Awakening in the Global Evolution of Cultures," in *Doors of Understanding: Conversations in Global Spirituality, in Honor of Ewert Cousins*. Steven Chase, ed. Quincy, IL: Franciscan Press, 1997, 335–356.

Gaylin, Williard. *Feelings: Our Vital Signs*. New York: Harper & Row, 1979.

———. *The Rage Within: Anger in Modern Life*. New York: Simon & Schuster, 1984.

Gebara, Ivone. *Out of the Depths: Women's Experience of Evil and Salvation*. Minneapolis: Fortress Press, 2002.

Gill, James J. and Linda Amadeo. "Anger, Hostility, and Aggression: How to Deal with Them in Ourselves and in Others," in *Human Development*, Summer 1980, 36–42.

Gilligan, Carol. *In a Different Voice*. Cambridge: Harvard University Press, 1982.

Girard, Rene. *Violence and the Sacred*. Baltimore, MD: John Hopkins University Press, 1977.

Gittler, Joseph B. (ed). *The Annual Review of Conflict: Knowledge and Conflict Resolution*, Vol. 2. New York: Garland Publishing, 1990.

Goodenough, Ursula. *The Sacred Depths of Nature*. Oxford: Oxford University Press, 1998.

Gottlieb, Roger S. *A Spirituality of Resistance: Finding a Peaceful Heart and Protecting the Earth*. New York: Crossroad, 1999.

Grant, Wendy. *Resolving Conflicts: How to Turn Conflict into Co-operation*. Rockport, MA: Element Books, 1997.

Gray, John. *Men Are From Mars, Women Are From Venus*. New York: HarperCollins, 1992.

Gregg, Richard B. *The Power of Nonviolence*. London: James Clarke & Company, 1960.

Habte, Jennifer S. (ed.). *The CMSM Shalom Strategy: A Manual to Promote Nonviolence, Reconciliation and Peacemaking*. Washington, DC: 1996.

Hahn, Thich Nhat. "Feelings and Perceptions," in *Nonviolence in Theory and Practice*, Robert Holmes, ed. Belmont, CA: Wadsworth, 1990.

Hall, Lavinia (ed.). *Negotiation: Strategies for Mutual Gain*. London: Sage, 1993.

Hammett, Rosine and Loughlan Sofield. *Inside Christian Community*. Washington, DC: Le Jacq, 1981.

Harpur, Tom. *Would You Believe?* Toronto: McClelland & Stewart, 1996.

Harre, Rom (ed.). *The Social Construction of Emotions*. Oxford: Basil Blackwell, 1986.

Harris, Amy Bjork and Thomas A. Harris. *Staying OK*. New York: Harper & Row, 1985.

Harris, Maria. *Proclaim Jubilee*. Louisville, KY: Westminster John Knox Press, 1996.

Hasling, John. *Group Discussion and Decision Making*. New York: Thomas Y. Crowell, 1975.

Haughton, Rosemary. *The Transformation of Man: A Study of Conversion and Community*. London: Geoffrey Chapman, 1967.

Helmstetter, Shad. *How to Excel in Times of Change: Turning Challenges into Opportunities*. London: Thorsons, 1992.

Henderson, Hazel. *Paradigms in Progress: Life Beyond Economics*. London: Adamantine Press, 1993.

Hessel, Dieter T. and Rosemary Radford Ruether (eds.). *Christianity and Ecology: Seeking the Well-being of Earth & Humans*. Cambridge: Harvard University Press, 2000.

Hillesum, Etty. *Etty, A Diary 1941–43* (Jonathan Cape, translator). London: Jonathan Cape, 1983. [Canadian edition: Klaas, A.D. Smelik (ed.). *Etty: The Letters and Diaries of Etty Hillesum 1941–1943*. Ottawa: Novalis, 2002.]

Hocker, Joyce L. and William W. Wilmot. *Interpersonal Conflict* (Third Edition). Dubuque, IA: William C. Brown, 1991.

Holmes, Robert (ed.). *Nonviolence in Theory and Practice*. Belmont, CA: Wadsworth, 1990.

Hopper, Paul. *Rebuilding Communities in an Age of Individualism*. Burlington, VT: Ashgate, 2003.

Hotelling, Kathy and Kathy H. Reese. "Women and Anger: Releasing in a Group Context," in *Journal for Specialists in Group Work*, 1983.

Houel, Alan and Christian Godefoy. *How to Cope with Difficult People*. London: Sheldon Press, 1994.

Houston, James. *The Transforming Friendship*. Oxford: A Lion Book, 1989.

Hunter, Doris. "On the Bhagavad-Gita," in *Nonviolence in Theory and Practice*, Robert Holmes, ed. Belmont, CA: Wadsworth, 1990, 16–19.

Izard, Carroll E. *Patterns of Emotions: A New Analysis of Anxiety and Depression*. New York: Academic Press, 1972.

Jackson, Timothy P. *The Priority of Love: Christian Charity and Social Justice*. Princeton: NJ: Princeton University Press, 2003.

James, William. "The Emotions," in *The Emotions*, Carl Georg Lange and William James, eds. New York: Hafner, 1967, 93–135.

Jandt, Fred E. (ed.). *Conflict Resolution through Communication*. New York: Harper & Row, 1973.

Jay, Ros. *Fast Thinking: Difficult People*. London: Pearson Education, 2001.

Jegen, Carol Frances. *Jesus the Peacemaker*. Kansas City, MO: Sheed & Ward, 1986.

Johnson, David W. *Reaching Out: Interpersonal Effectiveness and Self-Actualization* (Seventh Edition). Toronto: Allyn and Bacon, 2000.

Johnson, Elizabeth A. "Losing and Finding Creation in the Christian Tradition," in *Christianity and Ecology: Seeking the Well-being of Earth and Humans*, Hessel & Ruether, eds. Cambridge: Harvard University Press, 2000, 3–21.

Jones, Gareth. *Coping with Controversy: Helping Christians Handle Their Differences*. UK: Solway, 1996.

Jones, Hilary. *I'm Too Busy to Be Stressed: How to Recognize and Relieve the Symptoms of Stress*. London: Hodder and Stoughton, 1997.

Kassinove, Howard (ed.). *Anger Disorders. Definition, Diagnosis and Treatment*. Washington, DC: Taylor & Francis, 1995.

Kassinove, Howard and Denis G. Sukhodolsky. "Anger Disorders: Basic Science and Practice Issues," in *Anger Disorders: Definition, Diagnosis and Treatment*, Howard Kassinove, ed. Washington, DC: Taylor & Francis, 1995, 1–26.

Kidd, Susan Monk. *The Secret Life of Bees*. New York: Penguin Books, 2003.

Kilmann, R., M. Saxton and R. Serpa (eds.). *Gaining Control of the Corporate Culture*. San Francisco: Jossey-Bass, 1985.

Kimelman, Reuven. "Nonviolence in the Talmud," in *Nonviolent Theory and Practice*, Robert Holmes, ed. Belmont, CA: Wadsworth, 1990, 20–27.

Kolb, Deborah M. "Her Place at the Table: Gender and Negotiation," in *Negotiation; Strategies for Mutual Gain*, Lavinia Hall, ed. London: Sage Publications, 1993, 138–150.

Kornfield, Jack. *Buddha's Little Instruction Book*. New York: Bantam Books, 1994.

Krauss, Herbert H. "Intra-Psychic Conflict: A Conceptual Review," in *The Annual Review of Conflict: Knowledge and Conflict Resolution*, Volume 2. New York: Garland Publishing, 1990, 19–48.

Kressel, Kenneth, Dean G. Pruitt and Associates. *Mediation Research: The Process and Effectiveness of Third-Party Intervention*. San Francisco: Jossey-Bass, 1989.

Kriesberg, Louis. *The Sociology of Social Conflicts*. Englewood Cliffs, NJ: Prentice-Hall, 1973.

Lacoursiere, R. B. *The Life Cycle of Groups: Group Development Stage Theory*. New York: Human Service Press, 1980.

Landau, Sy, Barbara Landau and Darryl Landau. *From Conflict to Creativity*. San Francisco: Jossey-Bass, 2003.

La Haye, Tim and Bob Phillips. *Anger Is a Choice*. UK: Marshall Morgan & Scott, 1985.

Lange, Carl Georg. "The Emotions: A Psychophysiological Study," in *The Emotions*, Lange and James, eds. New York: Hafner, 1967, 33-90.

Lange, Carl Georg and William James (eds.). *The Emotions*. New York: Hafner, 1967.

Leaman-Miller, Kori. "Listening," in *Making Peace with Conflict: Practical Skills for Conflict Transformation*, Carolyn Schrock-Shenk and Lawrence Ressler, eds. Waterloo, ON: Herald Press, 1999, 59–67.

Leas, Speed and Paul Kittlaus. *Church Fights*. Philadelphia: Westminster Press, 1973.

Leas, Speed. *Moving Your Church Through Conflict*. Augsburger Press, 1985.

Lechman, Judith C. *The Spirituality of Gentleness: Growing Toward Christian Wholeness*. San Francisco: Harper & Row, 1987.

Leddy, Mary Jo. *Reweaving Religious Life: Beyond the Liberal Model*. Mystic, CT: Twenty-third Publications, 1990.

————. *Radical Gratitude*. Maryknoll, NY: Orbis Books, 2002.

Lerner, Harriet Goldhor. *The Dance of Anger*. New York: Pandora Press, HarperCollins, 1989.

————. *The Dance of Connection*. London: Piatkus, 2001.

Leviton, Sharon C. and James L. Greenstone. *Elements of Mediation*. Toronto: Brooks/Cole, 1997.

Lewis, C. S. *The Four Loves*. London: HarperCollins, 1960.

Lewis, Sperry Chafer. *He That Is Spiritual*. Grand Rapids, MI: Academic Books, 1967.

Lindberg, Anne Morrow. *Gift from the Sea*. New York: Vintage Books, 1975.

Lindenfield, Gael. *Managing Anger*. London: Thorsons, 1993.

Litherland, Alan. "Christianity," in *Peace Is the Way: A Guide to Pacifist Views and Actions*, Wright and Augarde, eds. Cambridge: The Lutterworth Press, 1990, 80–82.

Littlejohn, Stephen W. and Kathy Domenici. *Engaging Communication in Conflict: Systemic Practice*. Thousand Oaks, CA: 2001.

Lorenz, Konrad. *On Aggression*. New York: Bantam Books, 1966.

MacAskill, Ann. *Heal the Hurt: How to Forgive and Move On*. London: Sheldon Press, 2002.

MacGillis, Miriam Therese. "Re-inhabiting the Earth: Genesis Farm," in *Circles of Strength*. Helen Forsey, ed. Gabriola Island, BC: New Society Publishers, 1993, 11–19.

Mack, Raymond W. and Richard C. Snyder. "The Analysis of Social Conflict – Toward an Overview and Synthesis," in *Conflict Resolution Through Communication*, Fred E. Jandt, ed. New York: Harper & Row, 1973, 25–61.

Madow, Leo. *Anger*. London: George Allen and Unwin, 1972.

Malone, Janet. *Conflict and Anger in Women Religious*. (Unpublished Doctoral Dissertation), 1991.

————. "Gender Differences in Handling Conflict," in *Human Development*, Spring 1993, 11–15.

————. "Exploring Human Anger," in *Human Development*, Spring 1994, 33–38.

————. "Forgive But Don't Forget," in *Human Development*, Summer 1994, 5–8.

————. "Women and Self-Esteem," in *Human Development*, Summer 1996, 5–7.

————. "Improving Your Expression of Anger," in *Human Development*, Winter 1996, 26–29.

————. "The Helping Relationships," in *Human Development*, Winter 2000, 5–13.

————. "Prophets in Religious Life," in *Human Development*, Fall 2001, 34–40.

Manning, Marilyn and P.A. Haddock. "Temper Those Tantrums," in *Sky*, July 1989, 100–105.

Marum, Lori, Doreen Sterling and Willy Wolf. "Checking Ourselves Out: Power and Leadership in Community Work," in *Circles of Strength*, Helen Forsey, ed. Gabriola Island, BC: New Society Publishers, 1993, 61–66.

Marx, Robert. "Corporate Culture: The Rites and Rituals of Corporate Life," in *The Manager's Bookshelf*, Jon L. Pierce and John W. Newstrom, eds. New York: Harper & Row, 1988, 46–56.

Masheder, Mildred. "The Way to Co-operation," in *Peace Is the Way: A Guide to Pacifist Views and Actions*, Wright and Augarde, eds. Cambridge: The Lutterworth Press, 1990, 126–128.

Matthews, A. M. *The Seven Keys to Calm*. Toronto: Pocket Books, 1997.

Mayer, Richard J. *Conflict Management: The Courage to Confront* (Second Edition). Columbus, OH: Battelle Press, 1995.

McCullough, Michael E., Kenneth E. Pargament and Carl E. Thoresen (eds.). *Forgiveness: Theory, Research, Practice*. New York: The Guilford Press, 2000.

————. "The Psychology of Forgiveness," in *Forgiveness: Theory, Research, Practice,* Michael E. McCullough, Kenneth E. Pargament and Carl E. Thoresen, eds. New York: The Guilford Press, 2000, 1–14.

McFague, Sallie. *The Body of God: An Ecological Theology*. London: SCM Press, 1993.

————. *Super, Natural Christians: How We Should Love Nature*. Minneapolis: Fortress Press, 1997.

McKay, Matthew, Martha Davis and Patrick Fanning. *Messages: The Communication Skills Book*. Oakland, CA: Harbinger, 1983.

McKay, Matthew, Peter D. Rogers and Judith McKay. *When Anger Hurts*. Oakland, CA: New Harbinger, 1989.

Merton, Thomas. *Faith and Violence: Christian Teaching and Teaching Practice*. Notre Dame: University of Notre Dame Press, 1968.

Metz, Pamela K. and Jacqueline L. Tobin. *The Tao of Women*. Shaftesbury, UK: Element, 1995.

Milhaven, J. Giles. *Good Anger*. Kansas City: Sheed & Ward, 1989.

Miller, Francis. *Disputes: The "Square Root" of Disputes & Procedures for Settlement*. UK: Ruthtrek, 1998.

Miller, Jean Baker. *Toward a New Psychology of Women*. Boston: Beacon Press, 1976.

Miller, William Robert. *Nonviolence: A Christian Interpretation*. London: George Allen & Unwin, 1964.

Moore, Christopher W. *The Mediation Process: Practical Strategies for Resolving Conflict*. San Francisco: Jossey-Bass, 1996.

More, Thomas. *More's Utopia and the Dialogue of Comfort*. London: J. M. Dent & Sons, 1910.

Morgan, Gareth. *Images of Organization*. Newbury Park: Sage, 1986.

Muccigrosso, Robert. "Organizational Culture: Implications for Leadership," in *Human Development*, 1987, 8, 42–45.

Naisbitt, John and Patricia Aburdene. *Re-Inventing the Corporation*. New York: Warner Books, 1985.

Novaco, Raymond W. *Anger Control: The Development and Evaluation of An Experimental Treatment*. Lexington, MA: D.C. Heath and Company, 1975.

Nye, Robert D. *Conflict Among Humans: Some Basic Psychological and Social-Psychological Considerations*. New York: Springer, 1973.

Olmsted, Michael S. and A. Paul Hare. *The Small Group*. New York: Random House, 1978.

O'Murchu, Diarmuid. *The Seed Must Die*. Dublin: Veritas, 1980.

———. *Religious Life: A Prophetic Vision*. Ave Maria Press, 1991.

———. *Reclaiming Spirituality*. New York: Crossroad, 1997a.

———. *Quantum Theology*. New York: Crossroad, 1997b.

———. *Evolutionary Faith*. New York: Orbis Books, 2002.

Orbach, Susie and Luise Eichenbaum. *Bittersweet*. London: Century Hutchinson, 1987.

Origins: CNS Documentary Service. "US Bishops/ Framework for Action," December 1, 1994, 422–428.

———. "Northern Canada Bishops Responding to Family Violence," March 20, 1997, 633–638.

———. "John Paul II in Sarajevo. Replacing the Inhuman Logic of Violence with the Constructive Logic of Peace," April 24, 1997, 713–716.

O'Shea, Donagh. *Go Down to the Potter's House*. Michael Glazier, 1988.

Osiek, Carolyn. *Beyond Anger: On Being a Feminist in the Church*. New York: Paulist Press, 1986.

Panikkar, Raimon. *The Cosmopolitan Experience: Emerging Religious Consciousness*. Maryknoll, NY: Orbis Books, 1993.

Pax Christi USA. *Peacemaking: Day by Day*, Volumes 1 and II. Erie, PA: National Catholic Peace Movement, 1985, 1989.

Peachy, Dean E. "Choosing a Path for Conflict Transformation," in *Making Peace with Conflict: Practical Skills for Conflict Transformation*, Carolyn Schrock-Shenk and Lawrence Ressler, eds. Waterloo, ON: Herald Press, 1999, 91–100.

Pearce, W. Barnett. "Naturalistic Study of Communication: Its Function and Form," in *Communication Quarterly*, 1977, 25, 51–56.

———. *Communication and the Human Condition*. Carbondale, IL: Southern Illinois Press, 1989.

Pearce, W. Barnett and Stephen W. Littlejohn. *Moral Conflict: When Social Worlds Collide*. London: Sage, 1997.

Pelletier, Kenneth R. *Mind as Healer, Mind as Slayer. A Holistic Approach to Preventing Stress Disorders*. London: George Allen & Unwin, 1978.

Peters, Thomas J. and Robert H. Waterman. *In Search of Excellence: Lessons from America's Best-Run Companies*. New York: Harper & Row, 1982.

Peters, Tom and Nancy Austin. *A Passion for Excellence: The Leadership Difference*. New York: Warner Books, 1985.

Phelps, Joseph. *More Light, Less Heat: How Dialogue Can Transform Christian Conflicts into Growth*. San Francisco: Jossey-Bass, 1999.

Phelps, Stanlee and Nancy Austin. *The Assertive Woman*. San Francisco: Impact, 1975.

Pickthall, Mohammed Marmaduke (translator). *The Meaning of the Glorious Koran*. New York: New American Library (nd).

Pierce, Jon L. and John W. Newstrom (eds.). *The Manager's Bookshelf*. New York: Harper & Row, 1988.

Pinzon, Luis and Nestor Valero-Silva. *A Proposal for a Critique of Contemporary Mediation Techniques: The Satisfaction Story*. Hull, UK: The University of Hull, 1996.

Porter, Lawrence and Bernard Mohr (eds.). *NTL Reading Book for Human Relations Training* (Seventh Edition). Arlington, VA: NTL Institute Publications Department, 1982.

Prabhupada, Swami A.C. *Bhakivedanta. Bhagavad-Gita As It Is*. Los Angeles: Bhakivedanta B Book Trust, 1984.

Pranis, Kay, Barry Stuart and Mark Wedge. *Peacemaking Circles: From Crime to Community*. St. Paul, MN: Living Justice Press, 2003.

Quinn, Robert E. *Beyond Rational Management: Mastering the Paradoxes and Competing Demands of High Performance*. San Francisco: Jossey-Bass, 1988.

Quinn, Robert E. and Kim W. Cameron (eds.). *Paradox and Transformation: Toward a Theory of Change in Organization and Management*. Cambridge: Ballinger, 1988.

Redekop, Vern Neufeld. *From Violence to Blessing: How an Understanding of Deep-rooted Conflict Can Open Paths to Reconciliation*. Ottawa: Novalis, 2002.

Rex, John. *Social Conflict*. New York: Longman, 1981.

Richardson, Roy Franklin. *The Psychology and Pedagogy of Anger*. Baltimore: Warwick and York, 1981.

Robbins, Paul R. *Anger, Aggression and Violence. An Interdisciplinary Approach*. London: McFarland & Company, 2000.

Robert, Marc. *Managing Conflict from the Inside Out*. San Diego: University Associates, 1982.

Rohrer, Norman and S. Philip Sutherland. *Facing Anger*. Minneapolis, MN: Augsburger, 1981.

Rosenberg, Marshall B. *Nonviolent Communication: A Language of Compassion*. Encinitas, CA: Puddle Dancer Press, 1999.

Rubin, Jeffrey Z. "Conflict from a Psychological Perspective," in *Negotiation: Strategies for Mutual Gain*, Livinia Hall, ed. London: Sage, 1993, 123–137.

Rupp, Joyce and Barbara Loomis. *Rest Your Dreams on a Little Twig*. Notre Dame, IN: Sorin Books, 2003.

Russell, Peter. *The Global Brain Awakes*. Palo Alto, CA: Global Brain, 1995.

Rye, James and Nina Rye. *The Survivor's Guide to Church Life: How to Handle Relationships, Disagreements, Disillusion, Change.* Leicester, UK: Inter-Varsity Press, 1992.

Rye, Mark S., Kenneth E. Pargament, M. Amir Ali, Gary L. Beck, Elliot N. Dorff, Charles Hallisey, Vashuda Narayanan and James G. Williams. "Religious Perspectives on Forgiveness," in *Forgiveness: Theory, Research, Practice*, Michael E. McCullough, Kenneth E. Pargament and Carl E. Thoresen, eds. New York: The Guilford Press, 2000, 17–40.

Sagan, Carl. *Cosmos.* New York: Ballantine Books, 1980.

Sampson, Ronald. "Anarchism," in *Peace Is the Way: A Guide to Pacifist Views and Actions*, Wright and Augarde, eds. Cambridge: The Lutterworth Press, 1990, 59–61.

Sarton, May. *Anger.* New York: W.W. Norton and Company, 1982.

Schaef, Anne Wilson. *Women's Reality: An Emerging Female System in the White Male Society.* Minneapolis: Winston Press, 1981.

Schein, Edgar H. *Organisational Culture and Leadership: A Dynamic View.* San Francisco: Jossey-Bass, 1987a.

———. *Process Consultation, Volume I: Its Role in Organisational Development.* New York: Addison Wesley, 1987b.

———. *Process Consultation, Volume II: Lessons for Managers and Consultants.* New York: Addison Wesley, 1988.

Schell, David. *Getting Bitter or Better.* St. Meinrad: Abbey Press, 1990.

Schellenberg, James A. *Conflict Resolution: Theory, Research and Practice.* New York: State University of New York, 1996.

Scherer, Klaus R., Ronald P. Abeles and Claude S. Fischer. *Human Aggression and Conflict.* Englewood Cliffs, NJ: Prentice-Hall, 1975.

Schneiders, Sandra M. "Spirituality in the Academy," in *Theological Studies*, 1989, 50, 4, 676–697.

———. "Religious Life in a Postmodern Context," in *Religious Life Review* (RLR). January-February 2003, 42, 218, 8–30.

Schrock-Shenk, Carolyn. "Introducing Conflict and Conflict Transformation," in *Making Peace with Conflict: Practical Skills for Conflict Transformation*, Carolyn Schrock-Shenk and Lawrence Ressler, eds. Waterloo, ON: Herald Press, 1999, 26–37.

Schrock-Shenk, Carolyn and Lawrence Ressler (eds.). *Making Peace with Conflict: Practical Skills for Conflict Transformation.* Waterloo, ON: Herald Press, 1999.

Schutz, W. C. *Here Comes Everybody.* New York: Harper & Row, 1971.

Scott, Gini Graham. *Reolving Conflict with Others and Within Yourself.* Oakland, CA: New Harbinger, 1990.

Shannon William H. *Seeds of Peace.* New York: Crossroad, 1996.

Sharma, I. C. "The Ethics of Jainism," in *Nonviolence in Theory and Practice*, Robert Holmes, ed. Belmont, CA: Wadsworth, 1990, 10–15.

Sharp, Gene. "Nonviolent Action: An Active Technique of Struggle," in *Nonviolence in Theory and Practice*, Robert Holmes, ed. Belmont, CA: Wadsworth, 1990, 147–150.

Shinoda Bolen, Jean. *Crossing to Avalon: A Woman's Midlife Pilgrimage*. New York: HarperCollins, 1994.

Sider, Ronald J. *Nonviolence, The Invisible Weapon?* Dallas: Word Publishing, 1989.

Simon, Sidney B. *Getting Unstuck: Breaking Through Your Barriers to Change*. New York: Warner Books, 1988.

Simon, Sidney B. and Suzanne Simon. *Forgiveness: How to Make Peace with Your Past & Get On with Your Life*. USA: Warner Books, 1990.

Smedes, Lewis B. *The Art of Forgiving*. New York: Ballantine Books, 1996.

Sperry, Len. "Passive Aggression in Organisations," in *Human Development*, Summer 1990, 40–45.

Spong, John Shelby. *Why Christianity Must Change or Die*. New York: HarperCollins, 1998.

Starck, Marcia and Gynne Stein. *The Dark Goddess: Dancing with the Shadow*. Freedom, CA: The Crossing Press, 1993.

Stearns, Frederic R. *Anger: Psychology, Physiology, Pathology*. Springfield, IL: Charles C. Thomas, 1972.

Stokes, Gillian. *Forgiveness: Wisdom from Around the World*. London: MQ Publications, 2002.

Stratton, Jan. *Anger Management*. Romsey, UK: JPS, 1995.

Sutton, Ann. *Thriving on Stress*. Transatlantic Publications, 2000.

Swimme, Brian and Thomas Berry. *The Universe Story: From the Primordial Flaring Forth to the Ecozoic Era – A Celebration of the Unfolding of the Cosmos*. San Francisco: Harper San Francisco, 1992.

Tannen, Deborah. *That's Not What I Meant*. New York: Ballantine Books, 1986.

———. *You Just Don't Understand*. New York: Ballantine Books, 1990.

———. *Talking from 9 to 5*. New York: Avon Books, 1995.

Tavris, Carol. *Anger: The Misunderstood Emotion*. New York: Simon & Schuster, 1982.

Tavris, Carol and Carole Offir. *The Longest War: Sex Differences in Perspective*. San Francisco: Harcourt Brace Jovanovich, 1977.

Titmuss, Christopher. "Buddhism," in *Peace Is the Way: A Guide Pacifist Views and Actions,* Wright and Augarde, eds. Cambridge: The Lutterworth Press, 1990, 83–85.

Trigg, Roger. *Pain and Emotion*. Oxford: Clarendon Press, 1970.

Tuckman, B. V. "Development Sequence in Small Groups," in *Psychological Bulletin*, 1965, 63, 284–399.

Umbreit, Mark S. *Mediating Interpersonal Conflicts: A Pathway to Peace*. West Concord, MN: CPI Publishing, 1995.

Urquhart, Clara (ed.). *A Matter of Life*. London: Jonathan Cape, 1963.

Ury, William L., Jeanne M. Brett and Stephen B. Goldberg. *Getting Disputes Resolved: Designing Systems to Cut the Costs of Conflict*. London: Jossey-Bass, 1988.

Ury, William. *Getting to Peace: Transforming Conflict at Home, at Work, and in the World*. New York: Viking Press, 1999.

Van Doorn, J.A.A. "Conflict in Formal Organizations," in *Conflict in Society*, Anthony de Rueck and Julie Knight, eds. London: J. & A. Churchill, 1966, 111–132.

Van de Vliert, Evert. *Complex Interpersonal Conflict Behaviour: Theoretical Frontiers*. East Sussex, UK: Psychology Press, 1997.

Vanier, Jean. *Community and Growth: Our Pilgrimage Together*. New York: Paulist Press, 1979.

———. *Jesus, the Gift of Love*. London: Hodder and Stoughton, 1994.

———. *Finding Peace*. Toronto: House of Anansi Press, 2003.

Vella, Jane. *Learning to Listen, Learning to Teach. The Power of Dialogue in Educating Adults*. San Francisco: Jossey-Bass, 1994.

Viscott, David. *The Language of Feelings*. New York: Pocket Books, 1976.

Walton, Richard E. *Interpersonal Peacemaking: Confrontation and Third-Party Consultation*. Reading, MA: Addison-Wesley, 1969.

———. "How to Choose between Strategies of Conflict and Collaboration," in *NTL Reading Book for Human Relations Training* (Seventh Edition), Lawrence Porter and Bernard Mohr, eds. Arlington, VA: NTL Institute Publications Department, 1982, 62–65.

———. *Managing Conflict*. Reading, MA: Addison-Wesley, 1987.

Ware, James R. *The Sayings of Confucius*. New York: A Mentor Book, 1955.

Warner, Carmen Germaine. *Conflict Intervention in Social and Domestic Violence*. Bowie, MD: Robert J. Brady, 1981.

Warner, C. Terry. "Anger and Similar Delusions," in *The Social Construction of Emotions*, Rom Harre, ed. Oxford: Basil Blackwell, 1986, 135–166.

Weber, Richard C. "The Group: A Cycle from Birth to Death," in *NTL Reading Book for Human Resources Training* (Seventh Edition), Lawrence Porter and Bernard Mohr, eds. Arlington, VA: NTL Institute Publications Department, 1982.

Weeks, Dudley. *The Eight Essential Steps to Conflict Resolution: Preserving Relationships at Work, at Home, and in the Community*. New York: G. P. Putnam's Sons, 1992.

Wheatley, Margaret J. *Leadership and the New Science: Discovering Order in a Chaotic World* (Second Edition). San Francisco: Berrett-Koehler, 1999.

Whetten, David, Kim Cameron and Mike Woods. *Effective Conflict Management: Developing Management Skills*. London: HarperCollins, 1996.

Whitehead, Evelyn Eaton and James D. Whitehead. *Christian Life Patterns: The Psychological Challenges and Religious Invitations of Adult Life*. New York: Image, Doubleday, 1979.

──────. "Anger and Forgiveness," in *Seasons of Strength: New Visions of Adult Christian Maturing*. New York: Doubleday & Company, 1984, 115–128.

Wicks, Robert. "A Threat to Christian Communities: People Acting Passive Aggressively," in *Human Development*, Winter 1984, 7–13.

Wile, Daniel B. *After the Honeymoon: How Conflict Can Improve Your Relationship*. Toronto: John Wiley & Sons, 1988.

Williams, Emma and Rebecca Barlow. *Anger Control Training* (ACT), Parts 1,2,3,4. Bicester, UK: Winslow Press, 1998.

Williams, John Alden (ed.). *Islam*. New York: Washington Square Press, 1969.

Wink, Walter. *The Powers That Be: Theology for the New Millennium*. New York: Galilee Doubleday, 1998.

Woodward, Evelyn. *Poets, Prophets and Pragmatists: A New Challenge to Religious Life*. Notre Dame: Ave Maria Press, 1987.

Worchel, Stephen and Jeffry A. Simpson (eds.). *Conflict Between People and Groups: Causes, Processes and Resolutions*. Chicago: Nelson-Hall, 1993.

Worchel, Stephen, Dawna Coutant-Sassic, and Frankie Wong. "Toward a More Balanced View of Conflict: There Is a Positive Side," in *Conflict Between People and Groups: Causes, Processes and Resolutions*. Chicago: Nelson-Hall, 1993, 76–89.

Wright, Cyril. "Community," in *Peace Is the Way: A Guide to Pacifist Views and Actions,* Cyril Wright and Tony Augarde, eds. Cambridge: The Lutterworth Press, 1990, 129–131.

Wright, Cyril and Tony Augarde (eds.). *Peace Is the Way: A Guide to Pacifist Views and Actions*. Cambridge: The Lutterworth Press, 1990.